# The Quest of
# the Quiet Mind

## The Philosophy of Krishnamurti

P9-CNH-598

*by*

STUART HOLROYD

THE AQUARIAN PRESS
Wellingborough, Northamptonshire

First published 1980

© STUART HOLROYD 1980

ISBN 0 85030 231 5 (hardback)
ISBN 0 85030 230 7 (paperback)

Photoset by
Specialised Offset Services Limited, Liverpool
and printed in Great Britain by
Weatherby Woolnough Limited,
Wellingborough, Northants

## Acknowledgements

The author thanks the following for granting permission to quote from published works.

Victor Gollancz Ltd., Krishnamurti's English publishers, for quotations from his books, as listed in the Bibliography.

John Murray Ltd., for quotations from *Khrishnamurti: The Years of Awakening*, by Mary Lutyens.

Chetana Ltd., of Bombay, for quotations from books by and about Krishnamurti, as listed in the Bibliography.

# Contents

# *Introduction*

Averse as he is to any kind of labelling and the insidious ways in which language circumscribes reality, Jiddu Krishnamurti might well protest at being called a philosopher. Certainly most academic philosophers would object to his being so called, because he has read none of their books. In fact he professes to have read hardly anything, and in all his work there is scarcely a reference to any other thinker. Yet what else do you call a man who for more than half a century has pondered and discussed such subjects as freedom, death, fear, suffering, the purpose of life and the nature of intelligence? These are some of the perennial questions of philosophy, and Krishnamurti has expounded original ideas on all of them; ideas derived entirely from his own life experience.

But what an extraordinary life experience it has been; so extraordinary, indeed, that the teaching that has emerged from it (for, like it or not, Krishnamurti is a teacher) is probably too demanding and austere for the majority of people. In 1929 he declared it his purpose in life 'to set man free', and his prescriptions for the attainment of freedom and for the conquest of fear and suffering are simple indeed to comprehend but for most people difficult in the extreme to practice. His ideal of the human condition is that described in the lines of the poet T.S. Eliot:

> A condition of complete simplicity
> Costing not less than everything.

Krishnamurti himself was prepared to pay the cost, and in his early life was quite singularly situated to be able to do so, being provided for and protected from the harsher realities and the beguiling temptations of life in a manner befitting the young god that he was believed by many to be. His mode of life combined with a temperamental tendency towards mysticism to give him a number of religious experiences which at once enhanced his authority with his following and, paradoxically, caused him to repudiate that following, and which also served to lay the experiential foundation of his philosophy.

Krishnamurti has been expounding that philosophy, in books and talks, for well over half a century, and its lucid and challenging concepts have come to the notice of millions. If he had accomplished his declared aim, human beings would be fundamentally changed; so some may say that that aim was misconceived by a young man naive to certain realities of life and of human nature. But if he has not been a world-changer he certainly has been and remains a world-influencer, and in the 1970s a new generation, in revolt against materialism and with leanings towards the simple, spiritual life, fell under his spell. Though he has declared himself 'rather allergic to gurus', and insists that anybody can really learn anything of significance from nobody else, Krishnamurti's patent distinction as a human being and a philosopher has been such that over some three or four generations young people have flocked to listen to him. His world-wide influence is probably more profound than that of more flamboyant and well-publicized guru figures who have emanated from points East in recent years, and who generally are in the business of marketing some nostrum or technique for the alleviation of human malaise and the attainment of that spiritual growth that all but the most benighted of human beings ultimately come to conceive as the purpose of life. Krishnamurti has no nostrums or techniques to sell, or even to recommend. His only advocacy is of the love of truth. Philosophy, he says, 'means the love of truth, not love of words, not love of ideas, not love of speculations, but the love of truth. And that means you have to find out for yourself where reality is'.[1]

Let us, then, begin this short exposition and study of Krishnamurti's philosophy by seeing how this remarkable man found out for himself 'where reality is'.

[1] Numbers in the text refer to books listed in the Bibliography on page 91.

# PART ONE

## *An Extraordinary Life*

# I

It was a central belief in Theosophy, a religious movement established in 1875 by an American spiritualist, Colonel Olcott, and an energetic Russian emigré and occultist, Madame Helena Blavatsky, that at certain critical junctures in the history of the world a wonderfully wise and benevolent supernatural Being, the Lord Maitreya, had incarnated on Earth in human form. Once, he had incarnated in India as Sri Krishna, and on another occasion in Palestine as Jesus Christ. Theosophists further believed that the time when the Lord Maitreya, the World Teacher, would become incarnate again was imminent, and Madame Blavatsky sometimes said that the main purpose of the Theosophical Society was to prepare mankind for the coming of the World Teacher. This theme was taken up after her death in 1891 by another Theosophist of outstanding vitality and ability, Annie Besant, who later was to become President of the Society and to have what she considered the singular honour of being responsible for the upbringing of the World Teacher.

The actual discovery of the human being who was to become the Lord Maitreya was made by another remarkable Theosophist, a former pupil of Madame Blavatsky named Charles Leadbeater. One day in the spring of 1909 Leadbeater, who reputedly had highly developed psychic and clairvoyant powers, saw a group of Indian children bathing on the beach at Adyar near Madras, where the International Headquarters of the Theosophical Society was situated. He observed to a friend that one of these children had a quite remarkable aura, one which indicated that he would become a great spiritual teacher and orator. The boy was one of the four sons of a poor brahmin widower named Narianiah, who had a humble post working for the Society and lived in appalling conditions in a hovel of a cottage outside the compound. He was a weak, undernourished-looking child aged fourteen, and it certainly redounds to the credit of Leadbeater's powers of psychic perception that this unlikely boy should turn out to be the great spiritual teacher and orator Jiddu Krishnamurti.

The fact that he did so turn out, however, is partly attributable to Leadbeater's discovering him, and to the way that he and Mrs Besant brought him up, together with his brother Nitya. Narianiah, who was himself a Theosophist, was at first delighted that the leaders of the Society should interest themselves in the education of his boys. He was somewhat concerned about Leadbeater, who had a reputation for homosexuality, but he readily signed a document making Mrs Besant the boys' legal guardian. They were educated at Adyar, and then later in England, and in addition to general subjects were given instruction in the principles of Theosophy. Leadbeater and Mrs Besant soon decided that Krishna was to be the 'vehicle' for the new incarnation of the Lord Maitreya, and that their task was to prepare him for this role. Krishna learnt all about the Masters, those supernatural all-wise and all-loving beings whom initiated Theosophists claimed to be able to visit by means of astral travel, and he himself, under Leadbeater's tutelage, paid astral visits to and received instruction from a certain Master Kuthumi. His first publication was an account of the teaching he received in this way and was titled *At the Feet of the Master*.

Another of Leadbeater's alleged psychic endowments was the ability to divine past lives. In 1910 he started publishing in *The Theosophist* his *Lives of Alcyone*, which was an account of thirty previous incarnations of the boy Krishnamurti. His investigations revealed that the leading personalities in the Theosophical Society had worked together in previous eras, that 'Alcyone' had gone through his thirty incarnations between the years 22,662 B.C. and A.D. 624, and that there was an ancient prophecy that the Lord Maitreya would take possession of the body of Alcyone in order to bring His blessing upon the world. These revelations caused some friction among Theosophists, who vied with each other to identify themselves with the pseudonyms in the *Lives* and to claim past-life intimacy with the near-divine Alcyone.

Krishnamurti had always been a sensitive and religiously disposed child. After the death of his mother when he was ten years old, he reported several times seeing her spirit engaged in activities around the house. On 11 and 12 January 1910 he underwent his 'First Initiation', a ceremony organized by Leadbeater supposedly at an astrologically propitious time. In an account of it which he wrote to Mrs Besant, Krishnamurti told how he had left his body and gone into the company of the Masters, among them the Lord Maitreya and the Master Jesus, who had asked him a number of questions before solemnly admitting him to the Brotherhood of Eternal Life and giving him the Key of Knowledge. His report of the experience is very vivid, but whether it was an experience attributable to his psychic development or to his suggestibility must remain a moot point. What is significant is that the young Krishnamurti was clearly indoctrinated with Theosophy very thoroughly and was convinced of his own extraordinary destined role, for some of the key themes that he later developed are clearly a strong reaction against this indoctrination and conviction.

On the first anniversary of Krishna's initiation a prominent Theosophist named George Arundale formed an organization called the Order of the Rising Sun, dedicated to the single purpose of preparing the way for the ministry of the World Teacher. Some months later the organization was renamed the Order of the Star in the East and Krishnamurti was nominated the Head of the Order. On 28 December 1911 there was an occurrence that convinced many of the boy's divinity. A ceremony was held at Benares, during which Krishna was to give certificates of membership to people who had recently joined the Order. The procedure was not ritualized or charged with great religious significance. Members simply filed past the Head of the Order, who smiled and said a word of welcome to them as he handed them their papers. But suddenly the atmosphere changed so dramatically that the member approaching Krishna at the time involuntarily dropped to his knees and bowed his head to the ground. An observer wrote:

> All saw the young figure draw itself up and take an air of serene and dignified majesty, a stateliness new and strange ... A great coronet of brilliant shimmering blue appeared a foot or so above the young head, and from this descended, funnel-wise, bright streams of blue light, till they touched the dark hair, entering and flooding the head; the Lord Maitreya was there, embodying Himself in His Chosen.[22]

The written accounts of other witnesses of the scene are similarly ecstatic, and all tell how Krishna laid his hands in blessing upon the new members, bestowing upon them a smile of extraordinary radiance, tenderness and compassion. Leadbeater wrote that 'It was exactly the kind of thing that we read about in the óld scriptures, and think exaggerated',[22] and compared it with the Biblical account of the descent of the Holy Spirit at Pentecost. Subsequently 28 December was regarded as a sacred day by members of the Order of the Star in the East.

In 1911 Mrs Besant took Krishna and Nitya to Europe for the first time, and she travelled around giving a series of public lectures on 'The Coming of the World Teacher' and introducing 'Alcyone' to Theosophists. The Society had a number of wealthy and socially prominent members in England, and the two Indian boys were now given quite a different initiation than the one Krishna had undergone with Leadbeater: an initiation into the rituals and amusements of the English aristocracy. They were privately tutored, and their names were put down for places at Balliol College, Oxford, for the autumn of 1914.

After a brief return to India at the end of 1911, during which the above-related 'visitation' occurred, the boys were rushed back to Europe by Mrs Besant in order to get them away from their father, who was now threatening to have recourse to law to revoke Mrs Besant's guardianship of his sons. He brought an action in the High Court of Madras in March 1913, alleging an improper relationship between Leadbeater and the boys. After protracted hearings of evidence, the judge ruled that Krishna and Nitya should be made wards of court, which meant that they would have to return to India. Mrs Besant appealed against the decision, arguing that it would be against the boys' best interests to deprive them of the eduction that they were embarked upon, but the Appeal Court upheld the judgement of the lower court. A less determined person would have submitted at this point, but Mrs Besant took her appeal to the Judicial Committee of the Privy Council in London, who ruled that as the boys' wishes had not been consulted by the Madras Court its judgement was misconceived, and pointed out that if Mrs Besant had obeyed the Court's order she would have contravened the law of England by taking the boys out of the country against their will. The committee ascertained that the boys did not wish to return to India, and dismissed Narianiah's suit.

Mrs Besant's intention of having her protégés educated at Britain's most august university was thwarted, partly on account of the publicity given to the Court proceedings, but also no doubt because no Oxford college was keen to have among its alumni a young man who had been proclaimed a kind of messiah. The universities of Cambridge and London were equally circumspect, and Krishna and Nitya continued to receive most of their education from private tutors. The younger brother managed to pass his matriculation examinations and eventually to qualify as a barrister, but Krishna twice failed the examinations, which, however, did not prevent him from attending lectures at London University as an external student during the years 1917-18. In later life he often said that he was glad that his mind had not been conditioned by a formal academic education, but in youth he did his utmost to fulfil Mrs Besant's plans for him, and was disappointed by his academic failures.

While he was pursuing his studies, Krishnamurti continued as Head of the Order of the Star and wrote regular editorials for the Order's magazine, the *Herald of the Star*. By the early 1920s the Order had more than 30,000 members, and in 1921 some 2000 of them attended a Congress in Paris, at which Krishna spoke. He was now twenty-six years old, and was developing authority in his role. Mrs Besant wrote that on this occasion, 'he astonished all present by his grasp of the questions considered, his firmness in controlling the discussions, his clear laying down of the principles and practices of the Order'.[22]

One principle which he laid down particularly emphatically was that there should be no rituals in the Order of the Star. It was the first sign of his attitude of repugnance towards any kind of organized religious movement and towards all the pomp and mumbo-jumbo through which many religious leaders in the past had sought to buttress their authority. But Krishnamurti was not at this stage becoming sceptical of the organization and purposes of Theosophy. After attending a session of the League of Nations in Geneva, he wrote to a friend criticizing the insincerity and superficiality of the delegates, and said, 'I know how much better we Theosophists could manage the League of Nations, for I think we are more disinterested. You wait, when we get going we shall make a hum and beat them all at their own game.'[22]

The youthful combativeness and confidence of this are engaging, if scarcely consistent with the image of the budding World Teacher of surpassing wisdom. And likewise inconsistent with that image are several expressions of self-doubt and uncertainty that he put in letters to friends at this time. For instance, he wrote to Lady Emily Lutyens: 'I do a vague kind of meditation, but I must do it more rigorously and regularly. That's the only way. I don't know the philosophy of my life but I *will* have one ... I must find myself and then *only* can I help others.'[22] Clearly something quite exceptional had to happen to turn this man of twenty-six, with his sheltered background and with all the normal confusions and inner conflicts of a sensitive and intelligent person of that age, into an authoritative World Teacher, or even into the lucid and positive philosopher that Krishnamurti was to become.

## II

Something did happen, in August 1922, at Ojai in California. Krishnamurti later called it 'the process' and regarded it as the turning point in his life. He and Nitya arrived in California from the West, after travelling from Europe over a period of several months and attending Theosophical Conventions in India and Australia. There they had spent time with Leadbeater, who now boasted the title of Regionary Bishop for Australasia of the Liberal Catholic Church, a post which enabled him to indulge a taste for flamboyance in dress and ceremonial. Leadbeater had 'brought through' for Krishna a message from the Master Kuthumi which had a profound effect upon him. The message went:

Of you, too, we have the highest hopes. Steady and widen yourself, and strive more and more to bring the mind and brain into subservience to the true Self within. Be tolerant of divergencies of view and of method, for each has usually a fragment of truth concealed somewhere within it, even though oftentimes it is distorted almost beyond recognition. Seek for that tiniest gleam of light amid the Stygian darkness of each ignorant mind, for by recognizing and fostering it you may help a baby brother.[22]

Platitudinous though it was, this message seemed to Krishna very relevant to his condition at that time. 'As you know,' he wrote to Leadbeater, 'I have not been what is called "happy" for many years; everything I touched brought me discontent ... I did not know what I wanted to do nor did I care to do much; everything bored me in a very short time and in fact I did not find myself.' As a result of the message that he believed to emanate from the Master Kuthumi he began to meditate regularly, and a consequence of his meditation was, he wrote, that he 'began to see clearly where I had failed and where I was failing and ... began consciously and deliberately to destroy the wrong accumulations of the past years.'[22]

But 'the process' was not a deliberate intellectual assessment of himself and his life: it was an overwhelming physical and spiritual experience.

In his classic study, *Shamanism*, Professor Mircea Eliade tells how the shaman of primitive tribal religions was often 'a sick man who had succeeded in curing himself', and says that often the shaman's vocation was first revealed 'through an illness or epileptoid attack'. Furthermore, a characteristic of this revelatory illness is that the shaman experiences a separation from his physical body, and goes into a trance 'during which his soul is believed to leave his body and ascend to the sky or descend to the underworld.' It is some years since I read Eliade's book, but upon reading the accounts of Krishnamurti's 'process' I was reminded of it and prompted to look up these quotations, which are remarkably descriptive of what happened to him.

Both Krishna and his brother Nitya wrote accounts, and the two are complementary, the former giving a subjective view and the latter an objective one.

They had been staying at Ojai, about eighty miles north of Los Angeles, for some six weeks. Nitya describes Ojai at that time as a secluded and idyllic place, a narrow valley of apricot orchards and orange groves. It was through the General Secretary of the Theosophical Society in America, A.P. Warrington, that the brothers had been given the use of a cottage in the valley, and Warrington himself was staying in another cottage nearby. The reason for their stay was that Nitya had for some time been suffering from tuberculosis, and the climate at Ojai was said to be very beneficial for this condition. For part of their stay they had a pretty nineteen-year-old American girl named Rosalind Williams to look after Nitya, and she and Warrington both witnessed what happened to Krishna.

It started one evening, when Krisna developed a painful lump in the middle of the nape of his neck. The next morning he was found tossing about and moaning on his bed as if in great pain. Spasms of trembling and shivering possessed him. Rosalind would hold him for a while, which calmed him, but then he would suddenly push her away, complaining of terrible heat. He went on like this all day, with brief periods of calm and lucidity, and could eat no food. After a fairly tranquil night, the same condition continued all through the next day, which was a Saturday, in a more acute form, and on the Sunday he was even worse, showing little control of the trembling that shook his body, becoming conscious only intermittently and briefly, continually talking to people who were not there, and reacting hypersensitively to the slightest sounds.

The condition came to a climax on the Sunday evening. Just after the others had finished their evening meal, wrote Nitya, 'suddenly the whole house seemed full of a terrible force and Krishna was as if possessed.' He sobbed aloud, would have nobody near him, and complained vehemently about everything being dirty. At his urging, the others left the room and went out onto the verandah, where he presently joined them, but sat as far away as possible on a cushion on the floor, murmuring incoherently. Then, prompted by a suggestion from Warrington, he went and sat under a pepper tree just in front of the house, and there after a time he began to chant a mantram. The scene reminded Nitya of the story of the Buddha's illumination under the Bo tree. All three witnesses strongly felt that in these moments Krishna was visited by a Presence. 'The place seemed to be filled with a Great Presence,' wrote Nitya, 'and a great longing came upon me to go on my knees and adore, for I knew that the Great Lord of all our hearts had come Himself.'[22] Rosalind, although she had no background in Theosophy, spoke of actually seeing the

Lord Maitreya accompanied by other radiant beings: a vision which lasted about half an hour, after which she fell into a swoon. Krishna remained under the pepper tree, in samadhi, all that night and the next day, and on the evening of that day Rosalind saw three figures appear and take him away, leaving his physical body under the tree.

So goes Nitya's account. Krishna's own account of the experience of those three days relates the same sequence of events, and culminates with a paean of celebration of the visionary experience he had sitting under the pepper tree:

> When I had sat thus for some time, I felt myself going out of my body, I saw myself sitting down with the delicate tender leaves of the tree over me. I was facing the east. In front of me was my body and over my head I saw the Star, bright and clear. Then I could feel the vibrations of the Lord Buddha; I beheld the Lord Maitreya and Master K.H. [Kuthumi]. I was so happy, calm and at peace ... The Presence of the mighty Beings was with me for some time and then They were gone. I was supremely happy, for I had seen. Nothing could ever be the same. I had drunk of the clear and pure waters at the source of the fountain of life and my thirst was appeased. Never more could I be thirsty, never more could I be in utter darkness; I have seen the glorious and healing Light. The fountain of Truth has been revealed to me and the darkness has been dispersed. Love in all its glory has intoxicated my heart; my heart can never be closed. I have drunk at the fountain of Joy and eternal Beauty. I am God-intoxicated.[22]

Krishna later wrote to Leadbeater that after this experience he knew what he wanted to do and what lay before him – 'nothing but to serve the Masters and the Lord'. To another correspondent, his close friend Lady Emily Lutyens, he wrote: 'I am going to help the whole world climb a little higher than they are,' and he urged her to 'change, change with deliberation and a set purpose', apologizing for seeming to preach, but explaining that 'since I have changed and now that I consider that I have found myself, I want to help you realize your own self and to become great.'[22] And in these words he stated the fundamental purpose to which all his writing and talking over the next half century would be dedicated, though of course not in regard to Lady Emily alone but for anyone who cared to listen to him.

It was generally believed among Theosophists that

Krishna's 'process' was, as Leadbeater puts it, 'the preparation of that body for its Great Occupant'. The experience was not confined to those three days in August 1922 at Ojai, but was recurrent over the next eighteen months. During this period Krishnamurti travelled a great deal addressing gatherings of Theosophists, which he did with increasing assurance and authority. Although 'the process' caused him very great physical suffering, he did not once consider consulting a doctor about it, for he construed it in terms of the traditional concepts of Yoga philosophy and occult anatomy, according to which the process of evolution is accomplished through the opening or awakening of different *chakras*, or force centres, in the body, notably the *kundalini* centre at the base of the spine.

In August and September 1923, after a strenuous time presiding over the second international Star Congress in Vienna, Krishna spent some weeks relaxing in a village in the Alps near Innsbruck with a party of friends which included Lady Emily Lutyens and her daughter Mary, who was to become his biographer. In a letter to Mrs Besant, Lady Emily gave a vivid picture of Krishna at this time:

It is very curious to watch the phases through which Krishna passes. Sometimes he is just a frolicsome boy with apparently not a serious thought in the world. Then swiftly he changes and becomes the Teacher stern and uncompromising, urging his pupils onward towards swift progress. Again he is just tortured with the pain in his spine not speaking and just wanting quiet or most strange of all the figure that comes to dinner beautiful, with unseeing eyes merhanically eating his food and shrinking at every sound. Most beautiful of all when he sits in meditation chanting mantrams his soul going out in worship. These phases succeed each other in such swift succession that it is something of a strain to be always prepared for them.[22]

The pain in his spine could be understood as caused by the awakening of the *kundalini* force, although Leadbeater, who believed that his own *kundalini* had been awakened some years before, was at a loss to understand all the other symptoms that Krishna manifested: his behaving like one possessed, moaning, groaning and muttering incoherently; his extreme sensitivity to sound and revulsion to the touch of anyone; his loss of control of his body and tendency to fall over. It could be considered that the extreme form 'the process' was taking was commensurate with Krishna's unique destined role in the world, and Nitya even wrote to Leadbeater asking: 'Do you know at all if something similar to what is going on now was part of the preparation of the body of Master Jesus when the Lord came last time?' In reply, Leadbeater confessed: 'I don't understand the terrible drama that is taking place with our beloved Krishna.'[22] Nitya's interpretation, however, appeared to be supported by a message which Krishna himself 'brought through', ostensibly from 'the Masters', one night in November 1923. The message went: 'The work that is being done now is of gravest importance and exceedingly delicate. It is the first time that this experiment is being carried out in the world. Everything in the household must give way to this work, and no one's convenience must be considered, not even Krishna's. Strangers must not come there too often; the strain is too great. You and Krishna can work this out.'[22]

'The process' culminated in February 1924, in an experience which Krishna described in the following words: 'I had an extraordinary evening. Whatever it is, the force or whatever one calls the bally thing, came up my spine, up to the nape of my neck, then it separated into two, one going to the right and the other to the left of my head till they met between the two eyes, just above my nose. There was a kind of flame and I saw the Lord and the Master. It was a tremendous night.'[22] The yogic explanation of the experience that Krishna thus described would be, of course, that it was the opening of the 'third eye', or 'Ajna chakra', in the middle of the brow, which signifies the heightening of self-awareness and the expansion of mental powers, and the way that Krishnamurti's teaching developed after he had gone through 'the process' could certainly be cited as evidence to support such an explanation.

## III

As Head of the Order of the Star in the East, Krishnamurti became in the 1920s a man of property. In 1921 Baron Philip van Pallandt offered him as a personal gift his Castle Eerde at Ommen in Holland, together with an estate of 5000 acres of land, and Krishna accepted it on behalf of the Order, of which it became the headquarters. Then in 1923 an American benefactress bought for them the cottage at Ojai which he and Nitya found so agreeable, together with thirteen acres of land. In 1925, on a visit to his birthplace, Madanapalle in southern India, Krishna conceived the idea of establishing a university there, and the following year he was able to buy 300 acres of land in lovely country near the town, where a school was founded. With these and other properties, and with first-class world-wide travel provided for him and wealthy patrons to be found wherever he appeared, not to mention private incomes settled on him by Mrs Besant and the American benefactress, the Head of the O.S.E. had an enviable life. That many people should have been incredulous, and others aggrieved, when he later renounced his office and disbanded the Order, is hardly surprising.

A severe blow to Krishna's own belief in the O.S.E.'s purpose, and in the wisdom, power and benevolence of the Masters, must have been administered by the death of Nitya in November 1925. Krishna was on his way to India with Mrs Besant at the time, and when, on the morning of the 14th, she broke the news to him that Nitya had died in Ojai a few hours before, he was shattered, and so was his philosophy of life, the Theosophical view according to which Nitya had a vital function to perform in the ministry of the World Teacher. Only the day before, when he had received a telegram from Nitya saying that his illness had become more serious, Krishna had told a friend: 'If Nitya was going to die I would not have been allowed to leave Ojai', a statement of a degree of confidence and belief in the Masters which must have been severely shaken by his brother's death.

A tenet of the later Krishnamurti's teaching is that we should stay with our pains and sufferings, and should not employ thought and ideas as means of escaping from or alleviating them. According to his friend Shiva Rao, who shared a cabin with him during the voyage, Krishna stayed with his grief for ten days, during which time he was inconsolable, sobbing, moaning and hardly speaking to anyone, but then he appears to have emerged with a kind of intellectual reconciliation to Nitya's death, for he wrote: 'The pleasant dreams my brother and I had of the physical are over

... An old dream is dead and a new one is being born, as a flower that pushes through the solid earth ... On the physical plane we could be separated and now we are inseparable. For my brother and I are one. As Krishnamurti I now have greater zeal, greater faith, greater sympathy and greater love for there is also in me the body, the Being, of Nityananda.'[22]

The purpose of the trip to India was to attend the Theosophical Society Convention, which was held at Adyar from 24 to 27 December 1925. The following day, the 28th, was the fourteenth anniversary of the famous 'visitation' of the Lord Maitreya to the young Krishna, and on the sacred day an O.S.E. Congress was held. On this occasion there occurred an event even stranger than the 'visitation'. Krishna gave a talk to the assembly on the subject of the World Teacher, and suddenly towards the end of it, and in the middle of a sentence, the timbre of his voice changed and he began to speak in the first person. 'He comes only to those who want, who desire, who long,' he said, and then went on: 'and I come for those who want sympathy, who want happiness, who are longing to be released, who are longing to find happiness in all things. I come to reform and not to tear down, I come not to destroy but to build.'[22]

Mrs Besant was in no doubt as to what this dramatic change in Krishna's delivery meant. 'The coming has begun,' she told the Congress, and said that the event signified 'the final acceptance of the body chosen long before.' Krishnamurti himself seems to have believed in the Theosophical interpretation and, without any sense of personal pride, to have believed that he was serving as the vehicle for the Lord Maitreya. 'I personally feel quite different from that day,' he said, and compared himself to a vessel which had been so purified that 'anybody in the world can put a beautiful flower in it and that the flower shall live in the vase and never die.'[22] He was sure, he said, that the Lord would come again soon, and that it would be 'a nobler and far more beautiful occasion than even last time.'

The occasion when everyone expected another manifestation of the Lord through his chosen vehicle was at the next O.S.E. Convention, which was held in July 1926 at Castle Eerde, and was attended by some 2000 people. Their expectations were not disappointed. Again, towards the end of his address, Krishna broke into phrases of scriptural resonance couched in the first person. In the published version of his talks, they are even set out in blank verse:

> I belong to all people, to all who really love, to all who are suffering.
> And if you would walk, you must walk with me.
> If you would understand, you must look through my mind.
> If you would feel, you must look through my heart.
> And because I really love, I want you to love.
> Because I really feel, I want you to feel.
> Because I hold everything dear, I want you to hold all things dear.
> Because I want to protect, you should protect.
> And this is the only life worth living, and the only Happiness worth possessing.[1]

The question whether Krishnamurti was really literally inspired to make such pronouncements, and whether he uttered them spontaneously as he presumably would if they were the words of the Lord Maitreya, is a bit of a puzzle, particularly as they are printed in a volume titled *Early Writings*. One cannot but wonder whether there was not – perhaps at a subconscious level – an element of role-playing and even self-deception in the way that Krishnamurti was speaking at this time, which would explain the vehemence of his reaction three years later. In 1929 he spurned his followers, but in his 1926 Ommen talk he had said: 'I would make all of you drink at my fountain, I would make all of you breathe that scented air, so that you can yourselves become creators, geniuses, who make the world happy … For this reason you must awaken, you must walk along with me and follow.'[1] This was the sort of thing that Theosophists expected of the World Teacher, and however little sympathy one might have for the mentality of the blind follower, Krishnamurti's later repudiation of the response that he had so eloquently elicited does seem a little harsh.

At this time he was also advocating principles to which his later teachings were diametrically opposed. He was urging people to strive, to be ambitious in their aspirations towards the spiritual life, to pursue growth through disciplined efforts of the mind and will. 'Use your mind to drive you to your particular goal,' he urged the people at Ommen, and he told them, 'it is important, essential that you should understand with your mind.'[1] But two of the recurrent and central themes in his later teaching are that the operations of mind, of thought, serve only to confuse and obscure our perception of reality, and that deliberately to pursue the goal of personal development is a self-defeating enterprise, for it sets up conflicts which consume the energy needed for the very process of development.

That there should be discrepancies and turn-abouts in a man's thinking over the course of a lifetime is not a thing to be wondered at, but it does rather derogate from any claim to be privy to Revealed Truth or to speak with the authority of a Master. Most of Krishnamurti's utterances during the years 1926-27 tended towards the mystical and rapturous, and contrast conspicuously with his later, lucid, spare, no-nonsense manner. He spoke frequently of his experiencing union with 'the Beloved': an experience which clearly meant a great deal to him, though he was teasingly inexplicit as to what it meant for his followers. 'What you are troubling about,' he told them,

is whether there is such a person as the World Teacher who has manifested himself in the body of a certain person, Krishnamurti; but in the world nobody will trouble about this question. So you will see my point of view when I speak of my Beloved. It is an unfortunate thing that I have to explain, but I must. I want it to be as vague as possible, and I hope I have made it so. My Beloved is the open skies, the flower, every human being ... Till I was able to say with certainty, without any undue excitement, or exaggeration in order to convince others, that I was one with my Beloved ... I talked of vague generalities which everybody wanted. I never said: I am the World Teacher: but now that I feel that I am one with the Beloved, I say it, not in order to impress my authority on you, not to convince you of my greatness, nor of the greatness of the World Teacher, nor even of the beauty of life, the simplicity of life, but merely to awaken the desire in your hearts and in your minds to seek out the Truth.[1]

If he was somewhat ambiguous with his public, he was not so with his close associates. He wrote to Mrs Besant: 'More and more I am certain that I am the Teacher and my mind and consciousness is changed.' And to Leadbeater: 'I know my destiny and my work. I know with certainty and knowledge of my own, that I am blending into the consciousness of the one Teacher and that He will completely fill me up. I feel and I know that my cup is nearly full to the brim and that it will overflow soon. Till then I must abide quietly, and with eager patience ... I long to make, and I will make, everybody happy.'[22]

To make everybody happy is by no means a discreditable aim for a World Teacher, but it is quite a different matter from the purpose that Krishnamurti was proclaiming two years later: 'to set man free'. These years saw the great transition of Krishnamurti's life: from the mystic to the emancipator; from the gentle teacher with eloquent and extravagant turns of phrase to the stern moralist and trenchant castigator of all modes of human escapism, idleness, inauthenticity and self-deception; from the public figure revered by some and derided by many for being proclaimed the Christ become incarnate again to the very private figure, the *sanyasi*, the simple, solitary man without any attachments or pretensions.

What brought about the change? In one of his most revealing autobiographical passages, Krishnamurti explains:

Like everyone else Krishnamurti, in the past, searched, obeyed and worshipped, but as time grew, as suffering came, he wanted to discover the reality which hides behind the picture, behind the sunset, behind the image, behind all philosophies, behind all religions, all sects, all organizations, and to discover and to understand that, he had to hang on to a peg of unreality, of untruth, till, little by little, he was able to pass all those shrines that are limiting, that are binding, all the gods that insist on worship. In passing all those he was able to arrive where all religions, where all affections are consummated, where all worship ends, where all desire ceases, where the separate self is purified by being destroyed. It is because I have gone through those stages that I am able to speak with the authority of my own experience, with the authority of my own knowledge, and I would give to you of that knowledge, of that experience.[1]

Having arrived 'where worship ends', and having learnt to speak with the authority of his own experience and his own knowledge, Krishnamurti naturally felt himself in a false position as a figure whom people worshipped and looked to for guidance and understanding. Even Mrs Besant had declared

herself his disciple, and when she was present at his speeches
she no longer sat beside him on the dais, but sat on the ground
at his feet. In 1927 and 1928 Krishna's talks at O.S.E. and
Theosophical Society meetings showed increasing impatience
with such attitutes, and irritation with the way that he was
bound and limited by the image that people had of him.
'Because you have been accustomed for centuries to labels,
you want life to be labelled,' he told O.S.E. members.   'You
want Krishnamurti to be labelled, and in a definite manner, so
that you can say: Now I can understand – and then you think
there will be peace within you. I am afraid it is not going to be
that way.'[1]
     He foresaw that if his followers had their way a new religion
would be built up around him. 'You will build a temple,' he
predicted, 'you will set about forming rules in your minds,
because the individual, Krishnamurti, has represented to you
the Truth. So you will build a temple, you will then begin to
have ceremonies, to invent phrases, dogmas, systems of
beliefs, creeds, and to create philosophies. If you build great
foundations upon me, the individual, you will be caught in
that house, in that temple, and you will have to have another
Teacher come and extricate you from that temple, pull you
out of that narrowness in order to liberate you.'[1] Sometimes he
became severe almost to the point of insult in his efforts to
disembarrass himself of his following. 'How happy you would
be if I decided for you,' he told one gathering. 'You are all like
little children who cannot stand on their own feet and walk by
themselves. You have been preparing for seventeen years, and
you are caught in your own creation.'[1] And what, he asked,
would the people of the world at large care for the teachings of
Theosophy, and about the question of his own role and
identity which his followers set such importance on? 'The
people of the world are not concerned with whether it is a
manifestation, or an indwelling, or a visitation into the
tabernacle prepared for many years, or Krishnamurti himself.
What they are going to say is: I am suffering. I have my
passing pleasures and changing sorrows. Have you anything
lasting to give?'[1]
     Krishnamurti believed that he had something lasting to
give. He had his own experience and his own understanding of
life, and he had above all the knowledge with which to set man
free, but he could not convey it within the confines of the belief

system of Theosophy and the O.S.E., for liberation from all belief systems was the prerequisite of true freedom as he now saw it. So the next step that he had to take was the formal dissolution of the movement that had been building up around him for nearly two decades. It was a step that required an extraordinary resolution and courage: the courage to be a disappointment to thousands of people, to deny them the comfort and consolation that they had found in their beliefs, and to make them take a straight and undistorted look at the thing that for the most part they were least able and disposed to look at honestly – themselves.

Krishnamurti formally dissolved the Order of the Star at the Ommen Convention in 1929, on 3 August, with a speech delivered to a gathering of three thousand people. Explaining the reasons for his decision, he said:

> I maintain that Truth is a pathless land, and you cannot approach it by any path whatsoever, by any religion, by any sect ... Truth cannot be organized; nor should any organization be formed to lead or coerce people along any particular path ... Truth cannot be brought down, rather the individual must make the effort to ascend to it.[22]

Referring to his renouncing his position as Head of the Order, he went on:

> This is no magnificent deed, because I do not want followers, and I mean this. The moment you follow someone you cease to follow Truth. I am not concerned whether you pay attention to what I say or not. I want to do a certain thing in the world and I am going to do it with an unwavering concentration. I am concerning myself with only one essential thing: to set man free ... If there are only five people who will listen, who will live, who have their faces turned towards eternity, it will be sufficient ... Because I am free, unconditioned, whole, not the part, not the relative, but the whole Truth that is eternal, I desire those who seek to understand me, to be free, not to follow me, not to make out of me a cage which will become a religion, a sect.[22]

He urged his listeners to take a look at themselves and consider whether any real and fundamental change had taken place in them as a consequence of their being members of the O.S.E. and having heard Krishnamurti's talks over the years.

'You are all depending for your spirituality on someone else, for your happiness on someone else, for your enlightenment on someone else,' he told them, and

> when I say look within yourselves for the enlightenment, for the glory, for the purification and for the incorruptibility of the self, not one of you is willing to do it. There may be a few, but very, very few. So why have an organization? ... Those who really desire to understand, who are looking to find that which is eternal, without a beginning and without an end, will walk together with greater intensity, will be a danger to everything that is unessential, to unrealities, to shadows. And they will concentrate, they will .become the flame, because they understand. Such a body we must create, and that is my purpose.[22]

Mrs Besant and the leading Theosophists had often said that the teachings of the World Teacher, when he came among them, would probably be quite different from anything they had preconceived and hoped for, and that people should remain open to the new and the unexpected, but what Krishnamurti was now saying was so unexpected, and so incompatible with the teachings and prophecies of Theosophy, that they were unable to heed their own warnings and advice. Mrs Besant herself never made publicly known the disappointment and disillusionment she felt, but Leadbeater expressed the feelings of many when he delivered himself of the preposterous statement that 'the Coming has gone wrong'.


IV


Liberating himself from the incumbency of his position as Head of the O.S.E. and his public image as a messiah figure no doubt gave Krishnamurti great personal satisfaction and relief, but outwardly his life did not change very much. The properties of the Order were returned to their donors, but Krishnamurti continued to speak regularly to gatherings of people at Ommen, at Ojai and in India, although now these meetings were open to the general public. He was also invited to speak in many other countries and to widely varying assemblies of people, and invariably he accepted, spurred on by his desire to convey his experience of the joy of the totally liberated life and his prescriptions for its attainment.

In relation to his audiences, Krishnamurti gradually developed a unique manner and approach which was consistent with his refusal to be an authority and with his purpose of seeking out the few who would really listen to him and be helped by his experience to become liberated and creative themselves. 'Don't agree or disagree with what I say,' he would tell his audiences. 'Let us go into this together ... let us inquire ... look into it more deeply ... go slowly ... really look at it.' He was impatient with glib questions and premature conclusions, but always extremely courteous with the members of his audience, addressing each one as 'Sir', not out of deference but in order, by reversing the conventional speaker-questioner protocol, to keep them mindful of the fact that they were not there just to listen respectfully to the speaker but to participate in a dialogue and an inquiry.

Krishnamurti's own investigation of the many aspects of the Truth that he had discovered went on for many years, and different aspects were given prominence at different times as the circumstances of life – both of his own life and of life in the world at large – determined. His talks and writings of the 1930s and later were not simply expository, however, but were struggling attempts to render as clearly and precisely as possible the results of his experience and his investigations. This was no easy task, for 'truth is a pathless land', and language, just like organizations, has a tendency to constrain and distort it. The experience central to Krishnamurti's developing philosophy of life was what he variously referred to as 'the death of the self', 'the disappearance of the "I"', or the annihilation of individuality achieved through union with life itself. The language capable of getting his meaning across eluded him, and even people eager to understand were perplexed by his attempts to express it, and sometimes suspected that his coveting and cultivating an experience of such an ineffable nature was a kind of escapism.

To one person who expressed such thoughts, and whose failure to understand distressed him, his friend Lady Emily Lutyens, he wrote an explanation and protest which gives an illuminating insight into the man:

I am sorry that you feel that way about what I say. The ecstasy that I feel is the outcome of this world. I wanted to understand, I wanted to conquer sorrow, this pain of detachment and attachment, death, continuity of life, everything that man goes through, every day. I wanted to understand and conquer it. I have. So, my ecstasy is real and infinite, not an escape. I know the way out of this incessant misery and I want to help people out of the bog of this sorrow. No, this is not an escape.[22]

We shall consider in the sequel the stages through which Krishnamurti went, and the concepts he formulated, in attempting to convey his fundamental perception and experience of life, but in passing we may note that one development which helped elucidate his thought in the early thirties was his ruminations on the nature of time and memory. And it is fascinating to note that his biographer says that at about this time he lost his memory of the past almost completely. This, she suggests, 'was consistent with his teaching that memory, except for practical purposes, was a dead-weight that should not be carried over from one day to another; death to each day was constant rebirth.'[22] Yes, indeed, but for a philosopher to carry consistency between his thought and his life to such lengths is surely very extraordinary.

Mary Lutyens also tells us that in the course of his development Krishnamurti manifested psychic powers, particularly clairvoyance and the ability to effect healings, but he sought to suppress them, for he regarded the exercise of clairvoyance as an intrusion of privacy and did not want to become known as a healer because he did not want people to come to him just for physical healing.

The 1930s and '40s were decades when, as a great writer of the period, Thomas Mann, put it, 'the destiny of man expressed itself in political terms.' Total war, senseless violence, ideological tub-thumping, and political and economic debacles testified to the fact that human beings were pitifully deficient in the ability to foresee and control the consequences of their fears, greeds, envies and stupidities projected and magnified on the world stage. Political events dramatically demonstrated the disastrous results of things that Krishnamurti had attacked in the context of the O.S.E.: the follow-my-leader mentality, and the tendency of the human mind to seek the path out of its confusion by way of the ideological fixation of belief.

Krishnamurti now extended his diagnosis of the ills of man and society to the world at large, becoming the tireless advocate of what he considered the only revolution that could be effective in the circumstances: a radical transformation of human nature, an evolutionary great leap forward. Such advocacy was, of course, impugned as idealistic and unrealistic, but Krishnamurti knew from experience that the individual human nature could be radically transformed, and as all the world's troubles were obviously the projection of the failings of unregenerate man it followed that their solution could only be accomplished through such a radical transformation; and what was truly unrealistic was to expect change to be effected by administering more of the same medicine that had already been seen to aggravate rather than cure the ills of man and society: more organization, systematization and subordination of the aspirations of the individual to some myth of the ultimate collective good.

So Krishnamurti became identified in the minds of many with political anarchists, and he came under attack for having a negative attitude in a time that called for positive action. He replied to this charge:

> You who are always shouting at me for my negative attitude, what are you doing now to wipe out the very cause of war itself? I am talking about the real cause of all wars, not only of the immediate war that inevitably threatens while each nation is piling up armaments. As long as the spirit of nationalism exists, the spirit of class distinctions, of particularity and possessiveness, there must be war. If you are really facing the problem of war, as you should be now, you will have to take a definite action, a definite, positive action; and by your action you will help to awaken intelligence, which is the only preventive of war. But to do that, you must free yourself of the disease of 'my God, my country, my family, my house'.[23]

When the Second World War was over, leaving in its wake millions of dead, maimed and psychologically desolate human beings, Krishnamurti did not join with those who celebrated the triumph of right and the free world over tyranny and evil, nor did he share in the general mood of relief and euphoria. 'Has the war that is just over produced a deep fundamental change in man?' he asked. 'Have you fundamentally changed because of this present catastrophe? Do you not still call yourself an American, an Englishman, an Indian, a German and so on? Are you not still greedy for position and power, for possessions and riches? ... If you do not eradicate in yourself the causes of enmity, of ambition, of greed, then your gods are false gods who will lead you to misery ... You must pay the price for peace. You must pay it voluntarily and happily, and the price is freedom from lust and ill-will, worldliness and ignorance, prejudice and hate ... Humanity does not need more suffering to make it understand, but what is needed is that you should awaken to your own ignorance and sorrow and so bring about in yourself compassion and tolerance.'[23]

To the present day, a fundamental theme in Krishnamurti's talks has been that 'What you are, the world is', and he has urged the awakening to one's own ignorance and sorrow as the first step in effecting the transformation of the self and the world. Probably his most original teaching has been that such a transformation can and should be brought about immediately and is not something that is accomplished gradually through striving, seeking, and bringing one's life, conduct and thought by degrees more in conformity with some ideal. His prescription for this instant transformation is basically simple – to comprehend if not to practise – but in explaining it, Krishnamurti has developed a wide-ranging philosophy, complete with a metaphysic, an epistemology, an ontology and an ethic, which is quite a remarkable accomplishment for a man who professedly has read no philosophy, and according to his biographer would have forgotten it even if he had.

Krishnamurti does not believe that the necessary revolution in man and society can be achieved by modifying existing institutions, and he has been a vehement critic of all institutions, and of man's urge to institutionalize, ever since he himself escaped being turned into one. But there is one institution that he has not rejected entirely but has sought to modify and change for the better: the school. The creation of schools where children can be educated without being conditioned, without being insidiously inculcated with the prejudices and values of an unregenerate society, and can freely develop their own abilities, perceptions and ideas, has been Krishnamurti's practical work in the world, and several such schools now exist in India, America and England.

Since the dramatic and much-publicized events of the 1920s, Krishnamurti's personal life has been relatively simple and uneventful. He has been an ascetic, partaking neither of meat nor of alcohol, and has never married, and probably the main problem that people have with his teaching is that he demands of them a like asceticism and repudiation of the normal satisfactions and fulfilments of life. His own main satisfaction and joy appears to have been that of living in a state of heightened awareness and acutely responsive sensitivity to the natural world.

In the latter part of the year 1961 and early 1962, Khrishnamurti kept a daily diary of his experiences, observations, and the development of his thoughts, and many of the entries conclude with a report of his inner experience of 'the process', which, like forty years before, was causing him a good deal of physical pain and discomfort but at the same time seemed to be a necessary condition of a special state of consciousness in which he enjoyed a vision and experience of the world such as a child or a mystic might have. In this diary and in other writings Krishnamurti has passages of lyrical but at the same time precise observation that testify to the fact that a central idea in his philosophy, that of the importance of living and dying from moment to moment and thereby making awareness always new, is not merely a verbal formulation but is a straightforward description of a wonderful and lasting joy that may be experienced by anyone who has the courage and the single-mindedness to live according to Krishnamurti's philosophy.

Even those who do not have such courage and single-mindedness, who find the demands of asceticism too stringent, and the satisfactions of the physical life too essential and fulfilling to renounce, can nevertheless derive a good deal that is relevant to their living and thinking from the philosophy of Krishnamurti. So let us now consider what that philosophy is all about and wherein lies its originality.

# PART TWO

## *The Philosophy*

Super Star Guru : on the
downswing.
(not enough Charisma ).
or
Gout
after
tax-exempt.
ex-members        Waning)
writing exposes   Act of desperation
Create expectation.

Society Woman
Husband hates org.

Asst. - Advertising men.

Motorcycle 11 (Magazine)
18 in Study Room.
(Office)
I have to console myself that
the is divinely protected.

End - Motorcycle revving
and leaving.
Exercize - Heckling

# I

## On Human Bondage

To propose to set man free is a fine declaration of purpose for a philosopher, but not a particularly original one. Socio-political philosophers from Rousseau to Mill and Marx, existentialists from Kierkegaard to Sartre, and even a linguistic philosopher like Wittgenstein, who said his aim was 'to show the fly the way out of the fly-bottle', have all proposed a purpose similar to that declared by Krishnamurti in 1929. Where all philosophers of freedom differ, however, is in their ideas of human bondage, and it is in this respect that Krishnamurti's thinking is more radical than other philosophers', and utterly original.

Political philosophers generally take the view that human freedom is necessarily limited. The social contract is an agreement to surrender a portion of one's freedom in exchange for the benefits and satisfactions of living in an ordered society. And this exchange is regarded as a civilized thing, for the freedom we have to surrender to cement the social contract is the freedom to gratify and indulge such things as our selfish, acquisitive, vengeful or lustful impulses. We are on the whole pleased to have these impulses in ourselves and others constrained by the authority and power vested by virtue of the social contract in the law and its custodians. But the question of where precisely lie the limits of the rightful exercise of this authority and power is a vexed one, and people tend to have different ideas about it depending on whether they take the view that human nature is inherently good or inherently evil, and also depending on whether they themselves wield power and authority or have it wielded over them. And as people have different ideas about the subject, different structures of power and authority exist in different human societies, and these differences give rise to conflict, envy, ideology, persecution, politics and power-seeking. No wonder people come to the conclusion that the very idea of the social contract is unworkable, and seek to opt out of it, either by fighting their way to the top of the heap, where they can do as they like, or by trying to reclaim their liberties and to become self-governing and self-sufficient in as many aspects of life as possible.

Philosophers have discussed at length the pros and cons of such opting out, but it has been left to Krishnamurti to point out that the fundamental reason why the social contract is unworkable is not that people misconstrue or contravene its terms, but that the very idea of the voluntary surrender of freedom is a myth because the people who constitute our societies do not have any freedom to surrender, and that the very basic cause of their and the world's troubles is precisely this lack of freedom, this condition of bondage which for the most part they are unaware of.

It has been observed often enough that revolutions in human societies have only produced a reshuffling of the hierarchy, a new ruling elite, and in course of time in all but superficial effects, a restoration of the *status quo ante*. This tendency of human societies, whatever upheavals they may undergo, to stabilize along the lines of a rather predictable pattern, and moreover a pattern which is the antithesis of the declared aims of most well-meaning revolutionaries, testifies to the existence of some intractable element in those societies. And as societies are assemblies of human individuals it is probable that that intractable element is to be found in the individual. Could it be that, whatever they may profess, people do not really want freedom, or that they fear it?

From Dostoevsky to Erich Fromm, writers have argued that this is the case, and it is difficult to deny the proposition in the face of their evidence. But Krishnamurti points to another factor in the situation: that to be conscious of freedom negates the condition. As he puts it: 'If one says "I am free", then one is not free.'[9] This paradox takes us to the heart of Krishnamurti's concept of man, mind and consciousness, and we shall come back to it, but there is another paradox to note here: that although freedom is negated by our becoming conscious of it, it is by being conscious and aware of the modes of bondage that circumscribe and delimit our lives that we make possible the experience of true freedom. In this context we must not speak of the achievement of freedom, because according to Krishnamurti freedom is not something that can be achieved, for in seeking to achieve something there is striving, there is an element of time – the idea that something *is not* but *will be* – and there is dualism and conflict because the person conceives simultaneously an actual and an ideal state, and all these things negate true freedom.

It might be objected that Krishnamurti sets up a criterion of freedom which disqualifies from the condition all but a few rare souls such as himself. Few who listen to or read him on the subject can come away with more than a clearer recognition of their own unfreedom and an attendant feeling of dismay or acquiescence, although in that recognition there must be for some a stimulus towards personal change and growth, the shedding of some elements of inauthenticity in their lives and the establishment of a degree more integrity, or wholeness of being. Krishnamurti will not allow that authenticity, wholeness and freedom come by degrees, but he is surely not so widely read for the transformation that his teaching induces as for the insights it vouchsafes. And his insights into the varieties of human bondage are manifold and sometimes surprising.

'To be free,' says Krisnamurti, 'is not merely to do what you like, or to break away from outward circumstances, but to understand the whole problem of dependence.'[6] Or again: 'Freedom implies the total abnegation and denial of all inward psychological authority.'[11] Now, the idea that authority constrains individual freedom is clear enough, but we generally tend to think of that authority as something imposed and that works from without, and the idea of the existence of an 'inward psychological authority' which dictates our behaviour and our thinking, and even determines what we feel, see and experience, is another matter. Of course, it is not an entirely unfamiliar concept. Modern psychological and sociological studies have shown clearly that the techniques of 'conditioning' and 'thought reform' can plant in an individual an inward determining authority which directs his thinking and behaviour when he imagines that he is exercising his own free will. The cynical and exploitative use of such techniques has provoked many protests about the erosion of liberties and about the ethical implication of meddling with the human mind. But the problem goes deeper than that, for conditioning begins in infancy, and all the traditions, beliefs, ideas, and even the language, that we acquire from our social and cultural background only serve to constitute that inward psychological authority which keeps us in bondage.

'To see, you must be free from all authority, tradition, fear, and thought with its cunning words,'[8] writes Krishnamurti. The conventional wisdom regards man's development of language and rational thought as a glorious and evolutionary thing, but Krishnamurti regards these faculties with profound circumspection, for he sees them as a root cause of human bondage. 'We are lost, we are forlorn because we have accepted words, words, words ... You may give significance to life, you can invent as philosophers and theoreticians do, as religious people do – invent the significance of life, that is their job, but this is feeding on words when you need substance; you are fed with words, and you are satisfied with words.'[13] And such satisfaction, he implies, is inauthentic living, it is living in bondage, for the word is not the reality; the reality lies beyond the reach of words. It lies in simply seeing and experiencing, without allowing what is seen and experienced to be dwelt on by thought or interpreted by words. And true freedom exists only in the moments of such seeing and experiencing.

Thought is the real villain and tyrant in Krishnamurti's view of human bondage. One of his books is called *Freedom from the Known*, and the title expresses one of his most difficult propositions: that knowledge, which is based upon thought, is bondage. The proposition is difficult because it is virtually axiomatic in our thinking that knowledge liberates; but if you equate freedom with authentic and fresh seeing and experiencing, as Krishnamurti does, you can see how acquired knowledge and the processes of thought can diminish or even negate that authenticity and freshness.

Time has to be brought into the discussion, too, because knowledge is acquired in time, it depends on time because it is sustained by memory, which is the repository of things past; and also rational, linear thought goes on in time. Acquired knowledge and experience constitute one of the several kinds of inward psychological authority which limit our freedom, for they make us insensible to the new. The mind is burdened by the past, by expectations which are based on past experience and sustained by memory, and, so burdened, it is not free. Memory, the past, expectation and thought are all involved in a form of human bondage which anybody will acknowledge as such: fear. Fear arises when the pain and suffering of yesterday are carried over by thought, by expectation, to tomorrow; or again it arises when memory sustains and dwells on a pleasure or satisfaction and we fear losing it or not being able to enjoy it again; or when we contemplate what we are, what we have become in the course of time, and thought dwells on the vulnerability and ephemerality of this self which is a product of time and becoming. So pleasure, desire and death are things closely bound up with fear, and really to be free and to be without fear is not to be tyrannized by pleasure, desire and death.

Does this mean renouncing pleasure and desire, suppressing them? This is what most religions have advocated, even demanded, of their devotees. But renunciation and suppression do not lead to freedom, they lead to psychological division, contradiction and struggle, and thus they perpetuate fear; and Krishnamurti, who is not concerned with laying down codes of morality but with specifying the conditions of human freedom, does not teach renunciation and suppression. He proposes that by understanding the nature of pleasure and desire we might become free of their tyranny. Sensual pleasure, as a response to seeing or experiencing something beautiful, is a sensation which arises spontaneously and naturally, and such a response does not pose a problem, nor does it constitute any form of bondage. But when thought comes in, giving rise to the desire to possess, to hold on to, to perpetuate, then the perfectly natural reaction is perverted; and in this way pleasure itself is vitiated by desire.

It is important to distinguish in this context between thought and intelligence. To understand all the modes of dependence that bind us, we need to exercise great intelligence. 'Can you find out whether you are free from authority?' Krishnamurti asks, and he warns that 'it needs tremendous inquiry into yourself, great awareness.'[11] The quality that characterizes the truly liberated mind is that of 'choiceless awareness'. Awareness arises in the exercise of intelligence, but choosing is a function of thought. If, recognizing that desire is bondage, you choose and resolve not to desire something, what situation is created? Necessarily, it is a situation of conflict, because you have divided yourself into two persons, the one that desires and the one that vetoes the desire, and inward division and conflict precludes true freedom. It is only through intelligent choiceless awareness of one's modes of dependence that one becomes free. To ask, 'How am I to be free from dependency?' and to receive or conceive an answer to the question and proceed to do as that answer dictates, is also to create a situation of conflict. 'Whereas,' Krishnamurti writes, 'if you observe that a mind that depends must be confused, if you know the truth, that a mind that depends inwardly on any authority only creates confusion – if you see that, without asking how to be free of confusion – then you will cease to depend. Then your mind becomes extraordinarily sensitive and therefore capable of learning and it disciplines itself without any form of compulsion or conformity.'[11]

Any thinking that sets up internal conflict is, according to Krishnamurti, an obstacle to freedom; and he points out how much of our thinking is of this kind. Comparative thinking is, for instance; and comparative thinking is inculcated into us when we are very young. Children are told exemplary tales of heroes and saints, and urged to measure themselves up to these models, and all through our system of eduction, with its awarding of marks and passing and failing of examinations, we are made to compare ourselves with others. This, says Krishnamurti, is really a form of aggression and violence. 'Violence is not only killing or hitting somebody, it is in the comparative spirit. "I must be like sombody else", or "I must perfect myself". Self-improvement is the very antithesis of freedom and learning. Find out for yourself how to live a life without comparing, and you will see what an extraordinary thing happens. If you really become aware, choicelessly, you will see what it means to live without comparison, never using the words "I will be".'[11]

So ambition, which of course is a form of desire, is not the commendable and liberating thing that we are usually taught it is, for the moment we want to become something we are no longer free. 'The man who is ambitious, spiritually or otherwise, can never be without a problem, because problems cease only when the self is forgotten, when the "me" is non-existent,'[2] which is of course something that cannot occur in the context of comparative thinking. To revolt against the whole tradition of trying to become something, Krishnamurti says, 'is the only true revolution, leading to extraordinary freedom',[2] and to cultivate this freedom should be the real function of education: a function which unfortunately few educational institutions in our world perform, which is why thinking in terms of comparison, competition and becoming remains a fundamental and rarely questioned characteristic of our minds. Only when we are free of this kind of thinking can we really begin to learn, if we understand by learning not just the acquisition of knowledge but the discovery of the new.

It is not only the confusion of the human mind, which is inherent in its habitual modes of thought, that inhibits the experience of true freedom; it is also the pettiness of the mind's habitual preoccupations and its consequent insensitivity to the whole movement and processes of life in man and nature. 'The fundamental problem for the human being,' says Krishnamurti, 'is the question of freedom from "the little corner". And that little corner is ourselves, that little corner is your shoddy little mind. We have made that little corner, because our own little minds are fragmented and therefore incapable of being sensitive to the whole; we want that little part to be made safe, peaceful, quiet, satisfying, pleasurable, thereby avoiding all pain, because, fundamentally, we are seeking pleasure.'[13]

Krishnamurti's friend Aldous Huxley frequently made the point in his writings that the function of human sensory systems is to filter and limit the amount and the intensity of the experience that our minds have to deal with. Our sensory systems function to enable us to survive and work within our environment, and their sensitivity is geared to this requirement, although we know from the evidence of experiments with the effects of hypnosis and drugs that the filtering process can be inhibited, whereupon it is as if the flood-gates of sensory experience of and response to the world are suddenly thrown open. Thus to expand the mind, so that it is not confined to 'the little corner', is not fragmented and limited but is invaded by a sense of the wholeness of life, is to be liberated from a kind of physiological bondage, and various techniques for effecting such an expansion have been explored in recent decades.

Huxley advocated the controlled use of 'psychedelic' drugs like L.S.D, but Krishnamurti believes that there is too great a risk of dependence in such use and suggests that the same thing can be achieved by means of meditation. We shall consider his ideas and recommendations regarding meditation in a later chapter, for in the present context we are concerned with his insights into human bondage and freedom, and in this respect it is relevant to note the correspondence between his ideas of the truly free mind as the mind that gets out of 'the little corner' of the self with its preoccupations with pleasure and security, and the advocacy by Huxley and others of means of expanding consciousness. We know from these reporters from 'inner space' that the experience of expanded consciousness, however it is achieved, is analogous to a mystical or religious experience, and this fact throws light on one of Krishnamurti's more elliptical definitions: that 'a mind that is free is therefore truly religious.'[11] We could say alternatively that such a mind is not bound and limited by the separatist impulses of the human mind, but is an integral part of and responsive to the whole of life.

A very illuminating formulation of Krishnamurti's is that true freedom manifests in actions, not in reaction. 'Is not freedom *from* something a reaction and therefore not freedom at all?' he asks, and further: 'Is reaction away from anything freedom – or is freedom something entirely different from reaction, standing by itself without any motive, not dependent upon any inclination, tendency and circumstances. Is there such a thing as that kind of freedom?'[9] Of course, his contention is that there is such a thing, 'a state of mind which is so intensely active, vigorous, that it throws away every form of dependence, slavery, conformity and acceptance ... an inward state that is not dependent on any stimulus, on any knowledge.'[9] And he further maintains that only a person who is truly free in this sense is really capable of love. What we call love is generally a reaction, and our feeling love for somebody is dependent on this reaction being triggered by some physical characteristics, or combination of such characteristics, in a particular person.

But there is a kind of love, maintains Krishnamurti, that is not a reaction, not dependent on some particularity, but is purely an outgoing thing, a life force emanating from the inner centre of the self and which is not discriminatory as regards the objects that it relates to. But for such love to come into being a person must be free, which means that he must be a person who acts, not one who reacts, that he must have understood and transcended all the modes of human bondage and dependence, all outward and inward authority, all fear and conflict, and must furthermore have liberated his thinking and responding from the conditioning of past experience, which implies the suppression of memory and expectation. To accomplish all these things might seem to most of us to be work sufficient for a good part of a lifetime, but Krishnamurti's contention is that they cannot be accomplished progressively in the course of time but only *in toto* in the present moment. The question of how this transformation might come about has only been briefly touched on in the present chapter but will be taken up in a later one; but now let us turn to the subject of Krishnamurti's philosophy of mind and consciousness.

# II

## On Mind, Consciousness and the Self

The self-awareness advocated by Krishnamurti is something totally different from the self- and psycho-analysis of Freud and the psychiatrists, for the process of analysis implies the existence of a self that is analysed and another self which participates in the analysis, and in Krishnamurti's self-awareness there is no separation of, to use his terms, 'the observer and the observed'.

The Freudian view of human personality, with its hierarchy of the id, the ego and the superego, has profoundly influenced psychological thought in the present century, as have Freudian techniques of psychotherapy, in which 'reality testing' is employed as a means of adjusting the individual to the psycho-social norm. All this is anathema to Krishnamurti, who would say that a personality cannot realize wholeness and integrity of being from a starting point of a divisive and hierarchical view of personality, and who would regard any kind of adjustment therapy as something which both infringes and prevents freedom. Furthermore, the method of psycho-analysis, which involves working with memories and bringing the past into the present, can only achieve a stabilization of the self according to a pattern laid down by past experience, and if it manages to achieve such a stabilization it strengthens the false idea that the self is a permanent entity which develops individuality in the course of time through the exercise of the faculties of will, understanding and intelligence.

A practising psychologist and analyst once told Krishnamurti how a woman he had been treating for several months for severe depressions without success had gained a sense of release and ultimately a cure from attending a series of Krishnamurti's talks, and he wanted to know if Krishnamurti could recommend a method or technique which would not require the amount of time and patient investigation demanded by psychoanalysis, but would alleviate human miseries and depressions quickly. Krishnamurti did not answer the question directly, but asked the psychoanalyst what he tried to do with his patients, to which he replied that he tried to help them overcome their difficulties and depressions so that they could fit into society. To Krishnamurti's question whether it was important to help people fit into a corrupt society, the analyst answered that it was not his function to reform society or to try to create super-normal people. But, Krishnamurti persisted, 'if one is only concerned with helping the individual to conform to the existing social pattern ... is one not maintaining the very causes that make for frustration, misery and destruction?'[4] Psychoanalysis, apparently, was not concerned with the total development of man, but only with a part of his consciousness, but it was surely obvious that to attempt to treat a part without having an understanding of the whole that it was a part of could actually cause other kinds of trouble or disease. The analyst admitted that there was something in this argument, and that his profession tended to be too specialized and narrow in its view of man, but he repeated his question whether Krishnamurti could recommend a method or technique of therapy, not realizing that the very question implied the narrow and superficial view of man that he had just admitted to be wrong. 'Can a method or technique set man free?' Krishnamurti asked, 'or will it merely shape him to a desired end?' No reply from the analyst is on record, but the discussion up to this point clearly brings out the difference between Krishnamurti's psychological ideas and those of modern orthodox psychologists.

Over the last hundred years or so, psychological thought has made much of the distinction between the conscious and the unconscious or subconcious mind, and there has been a strong bias in this thought, largely through the influence of Freud, to regard the unconscious as a realm of chaos, disorder, and destructive and disruptive passions which needs to be brought under the control of the rational consciousness. Psychologists speak of the 'threshold' of consciousness and propose that all that is above this threshold is accessible to introspection and all that is below it is not so accessible but requires some special technique such as dream interpretation to make it so.

Krishnamurti makes use of the distinction between the conscious and the unconscious, but without the bias and the dichotomous tendency of the orthodox Freudian view. He prefers to speak of the different layers or levels of the mind, and he asks: 'Is the conscious mind different from the unconscious mind? We have divided the conscious from the unconscious; is this justified? Is this true? Is there such a division ... a definite barrier, a line where the conscious ends and the unconscious begins?'[2] To say that we are aware of our unconscious does not make sense, and as the unconscious is not a datum of our experience the term is really only an aid to our thinking and talking about the mind, and the division between the two aspects of mind is a projection out of our inherent confusion, a reflection of our divisive habits of thought.

If we speak of the levels of the mind, one thing we can observe is that the upper levels have been educated, trained, disciplined, conditioned according to the dictates of our reason, which is itself dictated to by society, culture and what we conceive as our needs. 'Is the unconscious, the deeper layer, uneducated?' Krishnamurti asks, and he answers the question in the affirmative, but he does not deplore the fact and call for the extension of rational understanding and control to the deeper layers, but on the contrary regards it as a good thing that these layers should remain uneducated, for: 'In the deeper layers there may be the source and means of finding out new things, because the superficial layers have become mechanical, they are conditioned, repetitive, imitative; there is no freedom to find out, to move, to fly, to take to the wind! And in the deeper layers, which are not educated, which are unsophisticated and therefore extraordinarily primitive – primitive, not savage – there may be the source of something new.'[11]

This affirmation of the unconscious and its processes, of the validity and use of the deeper levels of the mind, is one of the positive aspects of Krishnamurti's teaching. If we do not set up a purely theoretical barrier or threshold between the conscious and unconscious, he implies, we can encourage instead of inhibiting the flow of communication between the levels of the mind, and thus be more whole and spontaneous in our moment to moment living, and we will thereby become truly creative. Analytical processes cannot be creative in the deepest sense of the word, because creativity is an impulse of the whole being whereas analysis involves fragmentation and one fragment of the whole assuming authority over the other parts and the objectivity to examine them critically. 'Any exaggeration of any fragment of the whole consciousness,' says Krishnamurti, 'any emphasis on any fragment, is a form of neurosis,'[11] and exaggeration of the intellectual, analytical functions of the mind is as much a form of neurosis as exaggeration of emotional or spiritual aspects.

Human beings need a sense of individual personal identity, and sometimes they obtain this by identifying themselves with one of the fragments of the total personality. Then sometimes they may realize that such an identification is neurotic, or become dissatisfied with the narrowness and limitations of it, and seek to redress the balance by identifying themselves with many other fragments, with as many as possible in the hope of thus achieving wholeness, of integrating all the fragments. But if we stop to ask the question, 'Who is this entity that is trying to identify itself with the other fragments?' we see immediately that it is impossible to realize wholeness in this way, because the very idea that there is a separate self that can be identified with different fragments is a dualistic idea to start with, and that basic dualism is never resolved by the process of identification.

'There is in fact only one state,' Krishnamurti asserts, 'not two states such as the conscious and the unconscious; there is only a state of being, which is consciousness.'[2] So the next question is, What is consciousness? Is it something independent of its content, or is it entirely defined by and made up of its content? 'If consciousness is made up of my despair, my anxiety, fears, pleasures, the innumerable hopes, guilts and the vast experience of the past, then any action springing from that consciousness can never free the consciousness from its limitation,'[11] Krishnamurti says, and he proposes that the investigation of the question whether consciousness can ever empty itself of its content and be free is of supreme importance 'if there is to be a radical change in the human mind, and therefore in society.'[11]

If we attend to the functioning of the mind, we will realize that consciousness is always of the past. We are conscious only of things that are over. The psychologist William James coined the term 'the stream of consciousness', and the metaphor may be employed to elucidate Krishnamurti's thinking on this subject. Consciousness is a movement, a flow of mental events, and that flow is always from past to future, and at any moment the content of consciousness is so identified with this flow, so determined by the past and the future, by my memories and expectations, that the present is excluded from it.

Krishnamurti uses the analogy of a pendulum and proposes that the normal state of consciousness is a swinging backwards and forwards between the past and the future, which is a movement that excludes anything new because the future comes into being as a projection of the past, and although it may become slightly modified by the movement.it is really the past in another guise. Consciousness that is bound up in this movement is incapable of seeing a fact simply as a fact, and the question is whether consciousness can ever be something other than this movement which excludes the present. In the constant swinging of a pendulum there is an infinitesimal interval of complete stillness each time the pendulum reaches the extremity of its swing, and Krishnamurti suggests that the analogy applies in this respect too, in that in consciousness there are intervals between thoughts. 'Between two thoughts there is a period of silence which is not related to the thought process. If you observe you will see that that period of silence, that interval, is not of time, and the discovery of that interval, the full experiencing of that interval, liberates you from conditioning.'[2] To become focused upon these intervals, he proposes, is the meaning of meditation.

By way of illustration of his argument, Krishnamurti sometimes asks his audience whether a person who exclaims, 'How happy I am!' really is happy. 'The moment you are conscious you are happy, is happiness there?' he asks, and he argues that it is not, that the happiness we become conscious of is already past, and that the formulation of the thought, 'How happy I am!' is an instance of the swing from the past into a future determined by that past, and in which the present is annulled. This implies that when we really are happy, the very experience of that happiness is such that there is no room for consciousness of it, and it seems to imply that Krishnamurti sets little value upon consciousness and is advocating the cultivation of a state of mind that is somehow exclusive of or prior to consciousness. But, on the other hand, many of the people who are interested in his teaching are those who also commonly speak of the heightening or expanding of consciousness as an ideal, and it is relevant to inquire how Krishnamurti's apparent disavowal of the importance of consciousness can be reconciled with this kind of idealism.

Well, it can be reconciled, because what Krishnamurti is advocating is not the cultivation of an unconscious state, but of what he calls the silent mind, which comes into being when the mind empties itself of its content, of the known, and which is not a state of mindlessness but of intense and clear awareness of 'what is'. This awareness is not a movement of the mind. Movement is characteristic of the conscious mind, but the silent mind is free of movement although it is fully aware of the movements of consciousness. The silent mind can be aware of the stream of thoughts that flow through the conscious mind, but it does not discriminate between them in terms of value, importance or rightness; it just observes the flow. And this observation without judgement, this passive awareness or choiceless awareness of the flowing stream of consciousness is by no means a negative thing. In fact it can be very positive and effective in dealing with problems of any kind. It has the effect of breaking down the barriers between the different levels of consciousness, thus facilitating the flow between the unconscious and the conscious levels, and as a result of this, psychological problems tend to just go away, to become non-problems, and even practical or intellectual problems may yield a solution because the intuitive and creative faculties of the unconscious are given full and free play.

Krishnamurti's epistemology, then, consists in the postulation and investigation of a non-conceptual and non-dualistic mode of knowing, and in the assertion that it is only by means of this mode that we can know reality. And closely tied in with his thinking on this subject is his philosophy of the self.

The young Krishnamurti, as we have seen, had certain experiences, which he described as of union with 'the Beloved', and which clearly involved a sense of liberation from his individual consciousness and a merging with or participating in a higher and quite impersonal consciousness.

So real and all-important were these experiences to him that he could make such statements as: 'If you would understand, you must look through my mind. If you would feel, you must look through my heart',[1] with the implication that his mind and heart did not have the qualities of partiality, particularity and limitation that characterized other people's, but in some way participated in and were means of access to universality, and thus in a sense not really *his* at all. At this stage in his life, Krishnamurti had difficulty in elucidating his basic experiences and ideas. He would sometimes speak of liberation as the disappearance of the 'I' and at other times say that it consisted in the fulfilment or consummation of the 'I'. He would urge people to 'realize themselves and become great', or to 'die to the self'. But the verbal difficulties he had do not invalidate the experience that he was trying to describe the significance of; and that experience, which could equally truly if not very helpfully be described as the death of the self or the consummation of the self, remained a focal point of his later thinking.

Krishnamurti asks us to consider what the sense of the self consists in, and how it arises. In early infancy a human being does not have any concept of the self, and the first distinctions he makes between the self and the not-self relate only to the body. But the process that begins with distinguishing 'my hand' and 'my foot' extends by degrees to identifying a whole complex of feelings, experiences, thoughts, ideas, impulses, desires, memories, hopes, fears, etc., as 'mine', and this complex constitutes the self. When we examine these components of the self, however, we may suffer a blow to our pride, because they are all derived from our environment and culture, and the entire complex only comprises an individuality in the sense that the number of components and the ways in which they combine and interact is unique, which is not really a kind of individuality commensurate with the degree of self-esteem and sense of self-importance that most people have. This self, in fact, is just a bundle of perceptions and memories, but the more actions we perform imagining that it is the self that originates and executes them, the more substance we endow this really insubstantial entity with, and the more we come under the thralldom of the past. And as it gains substance, the self assumes authority, takes it upon itself to mediate between consciousness and reality, or rather

intrudes itself continually between the mind and *what is*, so
that it becomes a positive impediment to knowing.

Now if you say that the self is an illusion or a delusion,
many people will protest, feeling that their very identity and
existence is somehow threatened, but very likely many of these
same people will admit to a sense of dissatisfaction with the
self, a feeling that it is too limited, too undeveloped, and will be
looking for kinds of experiences that 'take them out of
themselves' or constitute an experience of 'self transcendence'.
This ambivalent attitude to the self, this simultaneous clinging
to it and wanting to be free of it, is very common, but for most
of us the self has taken on such substance and reality that the
proposition of its non-existence seems preposterous, and even
to seek and aspire to be free of it seems an absurdity, for we
wonder who is doing the seeking and aspiring if not the self.

'Can the "I" positively set about abnegating itself?'
Krishnamurti asks, and he proceeds to show that the task is
impossible: 'If it does, its motive, its intention, is to gain that
which is not to be possessed. Whatever its activity, however
noble its aim, any effort on the part of the "I" is still within the
field of its own memories, idiosyncrasies and projections,
whether conscious or unconscious. The "I" may divide itself
into the organic "I" and the "non-I" or transcendental self;
but this dualistic separation is an illusion in which the mind is
caught. Whatever may be the movement of the mind, of the
"I", it can never free itself; it may go from level to level, from
stupid to more intelligent choice, but its movement will always
be within the sphere of its own making.'[4]

So it appears that we are in a trap, that because of the
intrusion of the self we are cut off from the new and from
reality and condemned to a future which is but a projection of
the past. Is there no way out of the situation? Krishnamurti
believes that there is; through awareness, attention, through
practising the non-dualistic mode of knowing, we can become
self-less. And this means not only getting into a more
authentic relationship to *what is*, removing the screen between
consciousness and reality, but also overcoming such
tribulations of the human condition as fear, pain and
suffering, for these only exist as experiences of the self.

This last point needs to be elucidated, because it is a central
teaching of Krishnamurti's, and one in which he restates in his
own way the traditional Buddhist teaching on the overcoming

of sorrow, fear and suffering. All our troubles, he says, arise from our dualistic way of thinking, which makes us imagine that experiences are something we *have* rather than something we *are*, that there are two distinct entities, the experiencer and the experience, the observer and the observed. 'When there is no *observer* who is suffering, is the suffering different from you? You *are* the suffering, are you not? You are not apart from the pain – you *are* the pain. What happens? There is no labelling, there is no giving it a name and thereby brushing it aside – you are merely that pain, that feeling, that sense of agony. When you are that, what happens? Do you say you suffer then? Surely, a fundamental transformation has taken place. Then there is no longer "I suffer", because there is no centre to suffer and the centre suffers because we have never examined what it is.'[2]

Krishnamurti often uses the term 'the centre' for the self, and the term lends itself to an illuminating illustration of his ideas. A centre has space outside it, and that space is limited by the centre, it has a circumference determined by the centre. There is this centre, which has its own dimensions, borders within which it recognizes 'the me', and outside it there is a space, and although the centre may be able to expand this space – for instance, by taking psychedelic drugs – it cannot expand it very significantly but must always remain trapped in the limitations of its own making. As Krishnamurti vividly puts it: 'The little monkey may meditate, may follow many systems, but that monkey will always remain; and therefore the space it will create for itself will always be limited and shallow.'[11]

Most of our actions issue from the centre, and all our feelings and perceptions are qualified by the centre so long as we regard them as things we *have*. But there are times when suddenly we find that we are looking, living or feeling without a centre, although these times are usually of short duration because thought seizes upon the experience, dwells on it or wants to continue it, and this thought which is the past trying to project itself into the future becomes the new centre. We can, however, by practising passive choiceless awareness, begin to look, live and feel without the centre for longer periods without the noisy, opinionated and demanding self intruding and spoiling the experience. And this annulling of the centre, this death of the self, is not the awful end of everything that we might have feared when we first contemplated the prospect, because *life* goes on.

Life goes on but without the 'me' as the observer. Life goes on, the registration goes on, memory goes on, but the 'me' which thought has brought about, which is the content of consciousness, that 'me' disappears; obviously because that 'me' is limited. Therefore thought as the 'me' says 'I am limited'. It does not mean that the body does not go on, but the centre, which is the activity as the self, as the 'me', is not. Again that is logical because thought says 'I am limited. I will not create the "me" which is further limitation.' It realizes it and it drops away.[15]

Descriptions such as this, of the non-dualistic and non-conceptual ways of knowing and living, abound in Krishnamurti's talks and writings, and they are all means of trying to convey the nature and meaning of experiences which he has personally undergone. When we recall his descriptions of these experiences, and the quite considerable pain and suffering he went through, even as late as 1961 in the period covered by his *Notebook*, we are prompted to wonder whether the switch-over to the alternative mode of knowing, and the dissolution of the self as centre, necessitates or involves some actual physical change in the body. Krishnamurti would appear to believe that it does, that in some way the brain and its processes change, that even the neuronal firing of the brain cells ceases and established circuits of brain activity, of stimulus-response patterns, are wiped out. 'Can there be a mutation in the brain?' he asks, and answers: 'We say it is possible ... when there is a great shock of attention.'[17]

Whether this is what actually occurred in what Krishnamurti referred to as 'the process' must be a matter of conjecture, but we do know from recent researches in the electronic monitoring of brain activity that non-ordinary mental states, for instance of the meditator or the healer, have corresponding distinct brain states. The philosophical question whether mind and brain are distinct entities is not resolved by these observations, however, nor has Krishnamurti gone into it, though he has said that 'thought is a material process, a chemical process'.[17] This could be taken as a statement favouring what is known as the identity theory, according to which every mind-event or -state has its corresponding brain-event or -state and therefore there is no component of human personality antecedent to the development of the individual brain or that survives its death. This is a theory which, for obvious reasons, religious people find intolerable, so most religions incline to a dualistic view of man, as composed of a physical brain and a non-physical mind. As we have seen, however, Krishnamurti considers dualistic thinking as a block to the perception of truth, and the concept of 'wholeness' is central in his thinking, and indeed he does sometimes seem to be speaking from what is known as a materialist monist position, particularly in regarding thought and consciousness in terms of brain cell activity, but on the other hand he speaks of the silent mind generating no brain activity although it is intensely aware and in touch with reality, so to assign him to the materialist camp, as some critics have done, is to act on a partial and superficial understanding of his thought. Needless to say, Krishnamurti himself, who regards naming and labelling as pursuits of the dull mind, is indifferent as to what camp he is assigned to.

While we are on the subject of Krishnamurti's philosophy of mind, let us be clear about what he means by two terms which he frequently uses with rather special significance: memory and intelligence.

We have seen that Krishnamurti tends to regard memory as a primary cause of human bondage because it continually makes the future conform to the pattern of the past and thus prevents experience or perception of the new. But to understand this proposition clearly we have to distinguish between factual memory and psychological memory. My memory of any event may contain both components: the memory of precisely what happened, and the memory of the feelings or reactions I had with regard to the happening. When Krishnamurti proposes that the mind should be clear of its burden of memories he is not suggesting that factual memories should be expunged. Obviously our factual memories enable us to live and conduct ourselves in the world with such efficiency as we do, and although a person without them might have the joy of encountering the new at every moment, his moments would be few indeed unless he had somebody to look after him all the time. So we need our factual memories for practical purposes, but the trouble is that the human mind does not clearly distinguish between factual and psychological memories, and we tend to carry with us a large complement of the latter type, and it is with this battery of psychological memories that we meet life, meet every new situation and challenge, with the result that we always assimilate the new to the old and so never experience the novelty of it. When Krishnamurti advocates the clearing out of memories from the mind, it is these psychological memories, of past thoughts, feelings and reactions, that he is referring to.

A mind thus cleared becomes intelligent in Krishnamurti's sense of the term. To be intelligent has nothing to do with being knowledgeable. In fact, 'When you say "I know"', you are on the path of non-intelligence; but when you say "I don't know", and really mean it, you have already started on the path of intelligence. When a man doesn't know, he looks, listens, inquires. "To know" is to accumulate, and he who accumulates will never know; he is not intelligent.'[5] Nor has intelligence to do with intellectual or any other capacity. 'Capacity is not intelligence. Intelligence is sensitive awareness of the totality of life; life with its problems, contradictions, miseries, joys. To be aware of all this, without choice and without being caught by any one of its issues and to flow with the whole of life is intelligence.'[16]

True intelligence, then, consists in looking, listening, inquiring and being choicelessly aware. It is a function of the mind that is simple, in the sense that it is uncluttered with convictions, opinions, habits of thinking in terms of measurement or comparison. It is not personal, and it is quite different from thought. 'You may be very clever, very good at arguing, very learned. You may have experienced, lived a tremendous life, been all over the world, investigating, searching, looking, accumulating a great deal of knowledge, practised Zen or Hindu meditation. But all that has nothing whatsoever to do with intelligence. Intelligence comes into being when the mind, the heart and the body are really harmonious.'[13]

As intelligence comes of harmony, actions governed by it bring harmony into the world. Morality and virtue, then, are not the observance of precepts or principles, but consist in the spontaneous functioning of intelligence in the world, which 'naturally brings about order and the beauty of order'. And this, Krishnamurti concludes, 'is a religious life'.[13]

Which brings us to another major topic.

# III

*On Religion and the Religious Life*

Although Krishnamurti disparages all thought born of reaction or of past experience, it is difficult to conceive that his own thinking on the subject of religion was not profoundly influenced by reaction to his Theosophical upbringing and by his early experience of being regarded by thousands as the new Messiah, the vehicle of the Lord Maitreya. As we have seen, in the ecstatic experiences he had as a young man, Krishnamurti was quite convinced that he separated from his physical body and went into the presence of the Master Kuthumi and the Lord Maitreya, and actually discoursed with them and brought back pearls of wisdom from their lips. Reflecting on this years later, he acknowledged the vividness of the experience at the time and the conviction it had carried, but put it down to his suggestibility and the influence of the Theosophists, particularly Leadbeater. In his mature philosophy Krishnamurti leaves open the question of the existence of a supermundane world or dimension and of superphysical beings, and concerns himself with the psychology of religious belief and experience and with investigating what religion and the religious life really consist in.

Krishnamurti is fond of telling the story about God and the Devil seeing Man chance upon and pick up a shining object, which turns out to be Truth. God is delighted and remarks that the Devil is going to have a tough time now, but the Devil is unperturbed and says, 'Not at all; I'm going to help him organize it.' In Krishnamurti's view, the human mind's organizing tendency, which is a function of thought, is unconditionally an obstacle and impediment to the search for truth. No subject elicits his contempt – and he can on occasion be scathingly contemptuous – as surely as does that of organized religion and its devotees. He observes with

ON RELIGION AND THE RELIGIOUS LIFE 61

unarguable logic that man has been what he calls religious for millennia but is still bellicose, murderous, confused and petty. Religions, he concedes, have had some civilizing influence, but this is greatly outweighed by the mischief they have wrought in the world, by the cruelty and tyranny that man has imposed on man in the name of them, and by the falsehoods and cynical deceptions masquerading as divine truths and mysteries that they have foisted on people for the sake of maintaining priestly power and privilege.

He does not take the liberal attitude that a man's religion should be respected and that one of the fundamental human freedoms is the freedom of worship, and he is quite uncompromising – some would say uncharitable and destructive – when people protest, as some have done, that he is destroying their religion without putting anything in its place. He replies: 'What is false must be put away if what is true is to be.'[5] He remains unmoved when people say that through religion they have found comfort, understanding, love, or whatever. When a palpably good man described to him his devotional life and the joy he had in it, saying 'I spend my days in the shadow of God', Krishnamurti was unimpressed and asked, 'Isn't it important to find out if the shadow has any substance behind it?'[4] In such encounters, his simplicity and his logic cut through all forms of piety and complacency and are devastating.

The propositions that people must believe in something, and that a man without belief is somehow incapacitated for confronting life's problems and opportunities, would probably have the assent of most people, but in Krishnamurti's view they are dangerous clichés because they endorse a species of mental idleness that is crippling. 'Belief is one thing, reality is another,' he writes:

> One leads to bondage and the other is possible only in freedom ... Belief can never lead to reality. Belief is the result of conditioning, or the outcome of fear, or the result of an outer or inner authority which gives comfort. Reality is none of these ... The credulous are always willing to believe, accept, obey, whether what is offered is good or bad, mischievous or beneficial. The believing mind is not an enquiring mind, so it remains within the limits of the formula or the principle.[8]

There is a specious argument often used by religious proselytizers and apologists, and which for Christians particularly carries the weight of scriptural authority. It is that belief is a prerequisite of the revelation of the truth that is believed. 'Only believe, and you will see', they urge, and, echoing the Jesus of the Gospels, they harangue sceptics as 'Ye of little faith'. The story of the disciple 'doubting Thomas' is told in such a way as to elicit contempt for his reluctance to believe in what was by any standards a pretty incredible event. On the more sophisticated level there were theologians like Tertullian who argued that the Christian story was believable precisely because it was so impossible and absurd (*credo quia absurdum est*), and philosophers like Kierkegaard who advocated a 'leap' into faith when reason and logic proved incapable of ascertaining the truths of religion. So at all levels in Christian cultures this rather extraordinary proposition, that you will never know what to believe in unless you believe in it before you know it, has been promulgated, and reasonable people quite ready to concede that their mental endowment for apprehending truth is fallible have been persuaded by it to relinquish inquiry in favour of faith, hoping to reap a reward for their acquiescence, at the very least in an afterlife and hopefully in this life in the form of a marvellously fulfilling or revelatory spiritual experience.

Krishnamurti has no time for such casuistry, and by shifting the argument from the philosophical to the psychological plane he shows it up for the tendentious sophistry that it is.

Through experience you hope to touch the truth of your belief, to prove it to yourself, but this belief conditions your experience. It isn't that the experience comes to prove the believe, but rather that the belief begets the experience. Your belief in God will give you the experience of what you call God. You will always experience what you believe and nothing else. And this invalidates your experience. The Christian will see virgins, angels and Christ, the Hindu will see similar deities in extravagant plurality. The Muslim, the Buddhist, the Jew and the Communist are the same. Belief conditions its own supposed proof.[10]

Krishnamurti knew from experience what he was talking about. Had he not seen and conversed with the Master

Kuthumi and the Lord Maitreya when he had believed in them? The experience had been intoxicating and utterly convincing at the time, but it had not given him any grasp of ultimate truth. In fact it was only when he ceased to believe that he began to see things clearly. 'When the mind is free of belief, then it can look,'[10] he later said, implying of course that really being able to look at *what is* is the beginning of wisdom.

Another pious injunction open to the same criticism as the advocacy of belief is the encouragement of the spiritual quest in the terms, 'Seek and thou shalt find.' Naturally, Krishnamurti says, the human mind always finds precisely what it seeks; that is the trouble. Thought projects its own hopes, fears and longings, shuts its eyes and counts up to a hundred, then trots off in search of them; and finding them is no hard task because they never stray far from their origin and they want to be found anyway. That is the religious quest, but it is not the quest for truth, which is a quest that demands no preconceptions, no influence from hopes, fears and longings, and the total commitment of the free intelligence of an awakened and aware mind.

Again adopting the psychological point of view, Krishnamurti regards the religious quest, and the sanctification of it in legend and literature, as inspired by man's sense of mortality and existential loneliness and by the fear and confusion that this engenders. 'Man has always been seeking something beyond his own death, beyond his own problems, something that will be enduring, true and timeless. He has called it God, he has given it many names; and most of us believe in something of that kind, without ever actually experiencing it.'[13] But to embark upon such a search, Krishnamurti argues, is an illogical, quixotic enterprise, because if man did not know from experience what he was looking for he would not recognize it even if he found it, and if he did have experience of it he would not need to search.

Such an argument will seem to the religious as sophistical as the 'Only believe ...' argument appears to Krishnamurti, and no pilgrim of eternity is going to be turnd back by what he may regard as a logical cavil. But when Krishnamurti gets mischievous or scornful in argument, it is generally because he sees frivolity and superficiality in matters that demand commitment and seriousness. 'When you are enquiring into such an extraordinary question,' he told an audience in New

York in 1971, 'there must be the freedom of actually not knowing a thing about it. You really don't know, do you? You don't know what truth is, what God is – if there is such a thing – or what is a truly religious mind. You have read about it, people have talked about it for millenia, have built monasteries, but actually they are living on other people's knowledge, experience and propaganda. To find out, surely one must put aside all that completely, and therefore the enquiry into all this is a very serious matter. If you want to play with it, there are all kinds of so called spiritual, religious entertainments, but they have no value whatsoever to a serious mind.'[13]

The romantic attitude to man's religious aspirations sees in his 'divine discontent', his 'immortal longings', his persistent feeling that there must be something more to life and the universe than he has experienced, a kind of noble restlessness that drives him, like Goethe's *ewige weibliche*, 'ever onward and upward'. Krishnamurti takes a cool view of this attitude, remarking that 'in the demand for something more lies deception', and that 'deception is easy if one craves for some kind of experience'.[13] He asks how that craving arises, and suggests that it is because we get bored with our ordinary everyday experiences. Do people who aspire to a transcendental experience wonder whether such a thing exists? he asks, and again, how would they know if it they had one, lacking prior experience? The aspiration itself, whatever the poets and ecstatics may say, is, Krishnamurti believes, '*essentially* wrong', and in support of his contention he argues that the genuinely free person does not have it. 'I find that as long as the mind is in a state of fear, it wants to escape from it, and it projects the idea of the Supreme, and wants to experience that. But if it frees itself from its own agony, then it is altogether in a different state. It doesn't even ask for the experience because it is at a different level.'[13]

Devotion and worship are almost universally lauded practices, but like most other aspects of conventional religion they draw Krishnamurti's scorn. 'In ourselves we are so petty,' he says, 'So essentially nothing, and the worship of something greater than ourselves is as petty and stupid as we are. Identification with the great is still a projection of the small. The more is an extension of the less. The small in search of the large will find only what it is capable of finding.'[4]

The devotee who protests his love of the object of his devotion, and falls back on the argument that expressing such love gives him deep satisfaction and does no harm to others, does not get any concession or comfort from Krishnamurti, but only a barrage of rhetorical questions with implied negative answers: 'Is it selflessness to lose yourself in a book, in a chant, in an idea? Is devotion the worship of an image, of a person, of a symbol? Has reality any symbol? Can a symbol ever represent truth? Is not a symbol static, and can a static thing ever represent that which is living?'[4]

If these questions are not enough to discomfit the worshipper, there is an even more fundamental and devastating argument: that the worshipper is also the worshipped. One of the early Greek philosophers made the same point when he said that if a horse could conceive God he would conceive Him in the shape of a horse. Krishnamurti maintains that the object of worship, however abstractly it may be symbolized, must be a creation of thought, a projection of a person's hopes, fears, etc., as conditioned by his background: 'Your image is your intoxicant, and it is carved out of your own memory; you are worshipping yourself through the image created by your own thought. Your devotion is the love of yourself covered over by the chant of your mind.'[4]

When Mahatma Ghandi, in India in the 1930s, was speaking out against the tradition that only Brahmins could enter temples, Krishnamurti travelled around with him for some time and on one occasion was asked what he thought about this teaching. His answer was even more scandalous in the eyes of the faithful than Ghandi's proposal that anybody should be allowed in the temples. He said, 'God is not in temples, it doesn't matter who enters.'[17]

When the question arises, Is nothing, then, sacred? Krishnamurti recommends the questioner to try an experiment. Take a stick or a piece of stone, he says, put it on your mantelpiece and every day place a fresh flower in front of it, at the same time saying something like 'Om', or 'Amen'. Do this for a month, and you will see how holy that stick or stone has become, although of course only your devotion has made it so and it is not really different from any other you might pick up by the roadside. So the answer to the question is that nothing that is created by thought is sacred.

Krishnamurti's polemic is not against man's need for experience of the sacred, but against the stratagems he unconsciously employs to fulfil that need, and the unworthy objects that he cravenly allows to gratify it. 'Unless human beings find sacredness,' he writes, 'their life really has no meaning, it is an empty shell. They may be very orderly, they may be relatively free, but unless there is this thing that is totally sacred, untouched by thought, life has no deep meaning.'[17] And he puts the fundamental question, 'Is there something sacred, or is everything matter, everything thought, everything transient, everything impermanent? Is there something that thought can never touch and therefore is incorruptible, timeless, eternal and sacred?'[17] In his own experience there is, but its existence and nature are difficult to convey in words, which of course are the creation and the vehicle of thought, and thought has to cease before the sacred becomes manifest. Perhaps the most that can be said is that: 'That which *is*, is sacred.'[13]

In his *Notebook*, that illuminating record of his inner life and experiences over a period of several months, Krishnamurti makes a strong assertion of the existence of the sacred, although what he has to say about it will afford no sustenance for the God-hungry:

> There's a sacredness which is not of thought, nor of a feeling resuscitated by thought. It is not recognizable by thought nor can it be utilized by thought. Thought cannot formulate it. But there's a sacredness, untouched by any symbol or word. It is not communicable. It is a fact.
>
> A fact is to be seen and the seeing is not through the word. When a fact is interpreted it ceases to be a fact; it becomes something entirely different. The seeing is of the highest importance. This seeing is out of time-space; it's immediate, instantaneous. And what's seen is never the same again ...
>
> This sacredness has no worshipper, the observer who meditates upon it. It's not in the market to be bought or sold. Like beauty, it cannot be seen through its opposite for it has no opposite.[16]

Here we come to the positive aspect of Krishnamurti's philosophy of religion, after his devastating critique of its conventional forms and concepts. For all his strictures against believers, seekers, worshippers, ecstatics and enthusiasts, Krishnamurti himself is clearly a modern mainstream figure in the venerable Indian tradition of the holy man and teacher. No matter that he demurs, repudiates any following, and adopts Western modes of casual dress and occasional vernacular turns of speech, he is what all but the most bigoted sectarian would regard as a religious man. He is not a Christian, a Hindu or a Buddhist, although there is much in Buddhist philosophy that accords with his teaching, and Aldous Huxley even compared his talks and dialogues with the discourses of Gautama. So let us now see what he has to say on the positive side about religion and the religious life.

'We mean by religion,' Krishnamurti has written, 'the gathering together of all energy to investigate ... if there is anything sacred.'[17] And again: One has to investigate without any motive, without any purpose, the facts of time and if there is a timeless state. To enquire into that means to have no belief whatsoever, not to be committed to any religion, to any so-called spiritual organization, not to follow any guru, and therefore to have no authority whatsover.'[13] Being religious, then, implies dedication if not devotion, an intense dedication to investigating what is truth. Put aphoristically, 'The search for truth is true religion, and the man who is seeking truth is the only religious man.'[6] It may be objected that according to this definition there is no difference between the religious man and the philosopher, until we recall that the investigation into what is truth is not an intellectual exercise, a function of thought, but cannot begin until thought has ceased, until the self has been negated, and consciousness has been emptied of the impedimenta of memory, habit and conditioning. This work prior to investigation is more in the line of what is commonly acknowledged to be part of the religious life, for it involves total commitment, the recognition of an unregenerate state of being, and the exercise of certain faculties with a view to transcending that state.

But what faculties? The question again takes us away from what is conventionally regarded as the religious life. The regimens and disciplines of monks, who seek through them to coerce a recalcitrant and continually backsliding mind and body into the paths of godliness, are not advocated by Krishnamurti. 'Is the denial of pleasure or beauty a way that leads to a religious life?' he asks. 'Can a tortured, twisted, distorted mind ever find what is a religious life?'[10] No, because the very nature of discipline is the setting up of an inner conflict, the pitting of one set of desires against another, and as all desires are creations of the self and of thought, such conflict is the very antithesis of the religious life.

On one of his visits to India, Krishnamurti was visited by a man who had lived a rigorously ascetic life for thirty years, denying his body any kind of comfort, suppressing all desires, meditating long hours and fasting for days at a time. Despite all these disciplines, however, he found himself in a state of frustration, and said it was as if he had come up against a wall which would not be broken down; his mind could not reach beyond a certain point, yet he felt that there must be a stage beyond and that to reach it was the whole purpose of the ascetic life. He said he had talked to many other ascetics who had had the same experience of disappointment and frustration. Some believed that the breakthrough would eventually come through more arduous self-discipline and -denial, but this man felt that he would never get any further.

He was right, Krishnamurti said, no amount of effort could break down the wall. But perhaps he should consider a different approach to his problem. At present a part of his mind was trying to capture and dominate the whole, and even if it succeeded, that would not create a harmonious wholeness. He should ask himself whether it was not possible to approach the problems of life totally, with the whole of his being.

The ascetic confessed that he didn't really understand what Krishnamurti meant, and he wanted some direction as to what he should do. Krishnamurti said that he should not be concerned with doing anything, but only with discovering the feeling of the whole of his being, because 'this feeling has its own action'.[4] Right action would follow naturally when there was feeling without withholding, thinking undistorted by fear, and no seeking of a specific result. 'But,' said the ascetic, 'must not our desires be tamed?' Krishnamurti answered that to find truth required tremendous energy, and the deliberate suppression of desire produced inner conflict which dissipated this essential energy. So how, asked the ascetic, can one conserve energy? 'The desire to conserve energy is greed,' answered Krishnamurti. 'This essential energy cannot be conserved or accumulated; it comes into being with the cessation of contradiction within oneself.'[5] But should that not be attained, asked the ascetic, by the type of meditation he had been practising for years, by making the mind one-pointed? No, Krishnamurti said, 'such intensity is a hindrance to reality, because it is the result of limiting, narrowing down the mind through the action of will; and will is desire. There is an intensity which is wholly different: the strange intensity which comes with total being, that is, when one's whole being is integrated, not put together through the desire for a result.'[5]

The wall that the ascetic felt that he was up against was really his ego; it was the self, and all efforts of the self to break through its own barriers only served to strengthen those barriers. The understanding of the truth of this was the thing required to initiate a movement of the whole. The ascetic was grateful for the insight that Krishnamurti had given him, and he said in conclusion, 'My life has been an incessant struggle but now I see the possibility of ending this conflict.'[5]

This discussion is typical of many in which Krishnamurti expresses his conviction that to be religious means to think and act out the totality of one's being, which means out of a quiet mind, 'because only such a mind is a religious mind, sees the whole of life as a unit, a unitary movement ... [and] acts totally, not fragmentarily.'[13] Such a conception of the religious life rules out any distinction between it and the worldly life: a distinction that is made in all religions, but is a creation of thought with its divisive habits. In point of fact, anyone who considers himself to be religious or spiritual exhibits a mentality which is the very essence of worldliness. The same goes for anybody who disparages the material in favour of some idea of the spiritual, if only for the very practical reason that 'without the world of matter, the material world, we wouldn't be here.'[13] There is great beauty in the material world, and the enjoyment of it, through really seeing *what is*, is an integral part of the religious life, as is the understanding that to make of this enjoyment a centre, a focus of thought, is the surest way to kill it and to arouse those qualities that in many theologies are characterized as demons, for instance greed, lust, envy and despair.

In Buddhism and Christianity the quality which above all distinguishes the religious man is compassion, or love. It is for Krishnamurti too, but he does not regard this love as something that can be elicited by teaching, by precept, or by any kind of deliberation, for it consists in a spontaneous and unmotivated movement of consciousness towards the object. 'To be religious is to be sensitive to reality,' he has said, and 'from this sensitivity to the whole of existence springs goodness, love.'[6] And again: 'You can only find out what love is by knowing what it is not. Not knowing intellectually, but actually in life putting aside what it is not – jealousy, ambition and greed, all division that goes on in life, the me and the you, we and they, black and white ...'[6]

Religion, then, is incompatible with piety, with religiosity, with institutions and the institutionalizing mind; it is a way of being in the world, of seeing and relating to the world and its phenomena. It is not a yearning after the superhuman or the supermundane, but on the contrary is a realization of full humanness and of the sacredness of the mundane world, of *what is*. The religious mind is quiet, detached, non-seeking, non-believing, highly sensitive and creative. It is orderly and virtuous, and when it governs action it creates order and virtue, not in observance of moral fiats and prohibitions but because the action is an impulse within a harmonious and self-regulating totality.

All religions teach how to attain to the state that they represent as ideal, but Krishnamurti is original – some might say perverse – in insisting that to ask how is to automatically disqualify oneself from realizing the state, for the question presupposes the existence of a method or system, which there is not, and also that effort can achieve the desired result, which it cannot; and anyway, to desire a result is another disqualifier. So to the age-old question, What must a man do to be saved? – or to attain perfection, enlightenment, liberation, or to become godlike – Krishnamurti answers that there is nothing he can do. If this seems a melancholy message it must be understood that all doing is an activity of thought, which is bondage, and therefore to be free one must go by the path of not-doing, which is no easy task with the mischievous, chattering mind that man is endowed with. Although he declines to teach any system or method, Krishnamurti has a great deal to say about how, through meditation, the mind may become silent, and this is a subject we shall take up in the final chapter in the context of a discussion of the psychological revolution that Krishnamurti believes must occur if unregenerate man is not to destroy himself and the world.

# IV

## On Life and Death

Life is one thing, and living is quite another, and most of our problems, frustrations and dissatisfactions occur because our living is out of phase with the movement of life. Krishnamurti compares life to a great river, deep and wide, which flows continuously and steadily and in which there is always movement and activity, and he compares living, as it is for most people, to a little pool lying beside the river and unconnected with it, in which there is no movement at all and the water is stagnant. What most appear to want, he says, is 'little stagnant pools of existence away from life'.[6] The reason why they want this pool-existence is that they are more concerned with security and permanency than they are with life. In point of fact there is no security or permanency, so what they do in effect is forsake the real for the illusory.

Change, death and rebirth are the essential processes of life, observable in all the phenomena of nature, even in the cells of our own bodies, yet people often resent and seek to resist change and death. They seek security and permanency in family, property, status, reputation, habit, the observance of tradition, religion, and by circumscribing their lives with these ephemera they cut themselves off from the flow of life, with the consequence that they become insensitive, dull, and prone to all kinds of problems. But if we come to terms with the facts of change, death and rebirth, or rather learn to find joy in the sense of being a part of this immutable process of life; if we get out of our pool-existence and push out into the middle of the river, what happens? Then says Krishnamurti, 'life has an astonishing way of taking care of you, because then there is no taking care on your part. Life carries you where it will because you are part of itself; then there is no problem of security, of what people say or don't say, and that is the beauty of life.'[6]

Krishnamurti not only writes about the beauty of life, but

also expresses his sensitivity to it in passages written in a style of limpid lyricism. In several of his books, notably the *Commentaries on Living* series and his *Notebook*, he begins each short section with a description of the scene, the natural environment, in which the events or the discussion recorded took place. The descriptions are meticulous as to detail and imbued with feelings of delight and wonder in the natural world and its life. They precede passages of philosophical discussion, and they are not irrelevant garnishings to make the philosophy more palatable, but on the contrary are very effective illustrations of his basic teaching that only the uncluttered, silent mind really *sees* the world and is capable of an intensity of response and enjoyment which is never possible when thought enters.

These passages are highly poetic, and in passing it may be interesting to note that although Krishnamurti's ideas are original in their context several of our poets have expressed basically similar ideas. When John Keats wrote about the poet's 'negative capability' he was referring to the creative potential of what Krishnamurti would call the silent mind. When William Blake spoke of seeing 'not through but with the eye', he was advocating the kind of spontaneous and unconditioned seeing that Krishnamurti proposes; and one of Blake's 'Gnomic Verses' expresses Krishnamurti's philosophy of non-attachment and of flowing with life and renewing consciousness from moment to moment very succinctly:

> He who bends to himself a joy
> Doth the wingèd life destroy;
> But he who kisses the joy as it flies
> Lives in eternity's sunrise.

It is not irrelevant to point out these correspondences, because in a sense Krishnamurti's is a poetical philosophy. He often speaks about the creative and creativity as definitive properties of life itself. He is, however, no enthusiast for what we call the arts, for he considers that most literature, painting and music is not an expression of life but of the self of the artist. 'To be creative,' he writes, 'does not mean that we must paint pictures or write poems and become famous. That is not creativeness – it is merely the capacity to express an idea, which the public applauds or disregards ... Capacity is not creativeness. Creativeness is ... a state of being in which the self is absent, in which the mind is no longer a focus of our experiences, our ambitions, our pursuits and our desires. Creativeness is not a continuous state, it is new from moment to moment, it is a movement in which there is not the "me", the "mine", ... It is only when the self is not that there is creativeness – that state of being in which alone there can be reality, the creator of all things.'[2]

It could of course be argued that creativity is not as Krishnamurti describes it, that in fact conflict is of its essence – the Hegelian thesis and antithesis leading to a higher synthesis; and it has to be allowed that Krishnamurti uses the word in his own special way, in which it is virtually synonymous with his 'choiceless awareness'. Creativity, in his view, does not necessarily have any issue, produce anything, but consists in a state of mind that is capable of seeing and of affirming all manifestations of the processes of life, the destructive as well as the productive, in nature.

Another common word which Krishnamurti often uses with special significance is 'relationship'. He teaches the fundamental Buddhist principle that 'all of life is one', that all living things and processes are bound together in relationship. 'Living means relationship,' he writes, 'relationship means contact; contact means cooperation.'[13] But relationship must be a spontaneous process, a vital thing, which it often is not in human living because spontaneity gets hampered by thought. 'Have concepts any kind of significance in relationship?' he asks, implying that they have not. 'But the only relationship we have is conceptual ... There is an *actual* daily living and a conceptual living.'[13] In other words, our relationships with people and with things are generally based on images. People form images of each other as a result of the experiences of each other that they have in the course of time, and in every encounter they tend to react to the image rather than respond to the person. This is particularly true of marriage relationships, and Krishnamurti suggests a basic reason why many marriages fail or become dull when he asks: 'If I do not die to the *image* of myself and to the *image* of my wife, how can I love?'[12]

So again, the obstacles to authenticity are time and memory. Even a marvellous experience of spontaneous love, when it becomes a memory, can be an image that destroys relationship in the present. Krishnamurti suggests as a definition of the word relationship: 'to respond accurately'. So long as we respond to another person according to the image we have of him, we are not responding accurately, which means with care, with understanding, with love. And when people respond to each other inaccurately, according to an image, on the basis of past experiences of pleasure, hurt, desire, impatience, fear, disgust, disappointment or whatever, there is really no relationship, there is isolation; and in isolation there is no life.

Another thing which militates against the establishment and maintenance of vital relationships between people is the tendency of relationships to be based on dependence and mutual gratification, to be a kind of trading of qualities, perhaps based on the idea of complementarity, of the partners to the relationship making up for each other's deficiencies so that together they constitute a whole, although individually they are partial, incomplete. The incentive to the formation of such relationships is the need for security, not for experience of the fullness of life, so they lead to lives that are really little pool-existences à deux, still cut off from the river of life. And such pools can spawn all kinds of anti-life attitudes and behaviour, for instance of the man who tries to compensate for being ruthless and cruel in business by being loving and generous to his children, or of the man who seeks in his home and family a refuge from reality.

Krishnamurti has a good deal to say on the subject of relationship because it affords him the opportunity to expound the fundamental principles of his philosophy in the context of everyday human situations and problems. 'We are concerned with human problems, not with philosophies and beliefs,' he told a student audience at the University of California at Berkeley in 1970. 'We are concerned with human sorrow, the sorrow that most of us have, the anxiety, the fear, the hopes and despairs, and the great disorder that exists throughout the world.'[12] All human problems, he told the same audience, are interrelated, and if you understand one problem completely, then you understand all problems, and very often understanding is all that is required to dispel a problem. His manner of dealing with problems that people put to him is consistent with this principle. Some questioners have been disappointed because he has not given them a straight answer, but Krishnamurti considers that it is not his function to give answers but to investigate and help others investigate certain problems at depth. He declines to be an authority, and often for the sake of the discussion he speaks in the first person about a hypothetical problem situation, for instance in a marriage, and by means of this and other devices he leads the questioner into seeing how the particular problem that he is aware of is symptomatic of more fundamental problems.

Let us take an example. Here are some extracts from a reply Krishnamurti gave to a questioner who said: 'I am very seriously disturbed by the sex urge. How am I to overcome it?'

Sirs, this is an enormous problem ... Please bear with me if I do not tell you how to overcome the sex urge; but we are going to study the problem together, to see what is involved, and as we study the problem, you will find the right answer for yourself. First, let us understand the problem of overcoming ... That which can be overcome has to be overcome or conquered again and again ... Whereas, if you understand something, it is over ... So if there is a problem, as the questioner has, of sex, we must understand it and not merely ask: how can it be overcome? ...

Because all our pleasures are mechanical, sex has become the only pleasure which is creative ... I am not saying something extraordinary. Emotionally we are machines carrying out a routine and the machine is not creative ... So, as we are hedged all-round by the uncreative thinking, there is only one thing left to us, and that is sex. As sex is the only thing that is left it becomes an enormous problem, whereas if we understood what it means to be creative religiously and emotionally, to be creative at all moments ... surely then sex would become an insignificant problem ...

Another enormous thing which we have lost ... is love. Sirs, love is chaste and without love merely to overcome or indulge in sex has no meaning. Without love, we have become what we are today, mere machines ... Often we are emotionally driven without love, and what kind of civilization do you expect to produce in that way? ...

So, look at our lives and see what we have done. We do not know how to love. Our life is merely an aspiring for position, for the continuance of ourselves through our families, through our sons and so on. But without love what is our life? Surely, mere suppression of passion does not solve anything, neither the brutal sex passion, nor the passion to become something. Surely they are both the same. But a man who has real love in his heart has no sorrow and to him sex is not a problem. But since we have lost love, sex has become a great problem and a different one because we are caught in it, by habit, by imagination and by yesterday's memory which threatens us and binds us. And why are we held by yesterday's memory? Again, because we are not creative human beings ...

If you go into this problem and become aware of its significance you will see what it reveals – a series of imitations, a series of habits, a series of clouds, and memories – Most of the time we are enclosed in our own cravings, wants and fears, and naturally the only outlet is sex, which degenerates, enervates and becomes a problem. So, while looking at this problem, we begin to discover our own state, that is what *is*; not how to transform it, but how to be aware of it. Do not condemn it, do no try to sublimate it or find substitutions, or overcome it. Simply be aware of it, of all it means ... Then you will feel a new breath, a new consciousness, and the moment you recognize *what is*, there is an instantaneous transformation.[24]

These are only brief extracts from a long speech that Krishnamurti gave in answer to the question, but they illustrate how he gently and skilfully leads people out of narrow preoccupations with a particular problem into consideration of much wider issues; and often people find that this very movement and widened perspective *is* the answer to their problem, in that it results in the broader deployment of energies which formerly the problem consumed. They also illustrate how Krishnamurti relates problems to his basic philosophy of life and manages to convey aspects of that philosophy in his reply, for instance in this case his ideas on the subjects of authority, will, freedom, creativity, love, memory and awareness.

The principle that there is relationship between all things leads to the further point that Krishnamurti expresses in the title of one of his books, *You Are the World*. For all its emphasis on states of consciousness, Krishnamurti's is not a solipsistic or socially irrelevant philosophy. 'I think one has to understand,' he writes, 'that we are the world and the world is us. The world is each one of us; to feel that, to be really committed to it and to nothing else, brings about a feeling of great responsibility and an action that must not be fragmentary, but whole.'[13] So to deplore the mess that the world is in is an act of self-criticism, which should awaken self-

awareness and lead to transformation, both in the individual
and, by extension, in society.

Now one of the problems that we all have, and which is
often raised in Krishnamurti's discussion sessions, is of
understanding the purpose or meaning of life. We ask
ourselves, each other, or priests or philosophers, what the
ultimate significance or purpose of life is, and some people get
distressed, even to the point of suicide, if they find the question
unanswerable. Krishnamurti's view is that the question of
purpose *is* unanswerable, and that 'constantly to seek the
purpose is one of the odd escapes of man'[8] from the insecurity
and uncertainties of life, and from the realization, which is
hard to accommodate to the conditions of normal living and
attitudes to living, that 'all life is in the present, not in the
shadow of yesterday or in the brightness of tomorrow's hope'.[8]
People actually speak of *giving* life meaning or significance,
and, amazingly, they say it without any sense of irony,
although the very expression is an admission that this
significance is a creation of thought. 'When you say, "I have
no significance, there is no significance to life", it is thought
that has made you say there is no significance, because you
want significance. But when there is no movement of thought,
life is full of significance. It has tremendous beauty.'[17]

The perception and experience of significance comes of
really understanding and feeling that 'you are the world', and
of having become so completely divested of all the superficial
trappings of selfhood and free of all the fears and anxieties of
self-centredness, that you can commit yourself to the flow of
the river of life and go along with it. But this also means going
along with and being non-anxious about the fact of death.
Living and dying go together, says Krishnamurti, they are not
two separate things, and 'so one must enquire what it means
to die, because that is part of our living.'[13]

People who have gone to Krishnamurti suffering the grief of
bereavement have not been given the comforting assurances
that priests and clergymen offer in such circumstances. Once
in India a woman who had lost her husband and one of her
three children went to Krishnamurti in the company of her
uncle, a devout Hindu. The uncle said that none of the
ceremonies or beliefs of their religion had been able to console
the woman, and indeed when she told her story to

Krishnamurti she wept copiously all the time. When she had finished, Krishnamurti asked her is she had come to him because she wanted to talk about death and bereavement seriously or in order to be comforted by some explanation, to be distracted from her grief by some reassuring words. She said that she wanted to go into the subject deeply, although she didn't know if she would be able to face what he was going to say to her.

Krishnamurti asked the woman to examine her sorrow, and to ask whether it was for her husband or for herself. 'If you are crying for him,' he said, 'Can your tears help him? He has gone irrevocably. Do what you will, you will never have him back ... But if you are crying for yourself, because of your loneliness, your empty life, because of the sensual pleasures you had and the companionship, then you are crying, aren't you, out of your own emptiness and out of self-pity ... Now that he has gone you are realizing, aren't you, your own actual state. His death has shaken you and shown you the actual state of your mind and heart. You may not be willing to look at it; you may reject it out of fear, but if you observe a little more you will see that you are crying out of your own loneliness, out of your inward poverty – which is, out of self-pity.'[8]

This was cruel, the woman said, and there was no comfort in it for her. Krishnamurti replied that comfort was always based on illusion, and that the only way to go beyond sorrow was to see things as they really were, and that surely it was not cruelty to point this out. Death was inevitable for everyone, and 'one has to come into touch with this enormous fact of life'. At this point the uncle put in the protest that there is in everyone an immortal soul which goes through a series of incarnations until it achieves perfection. Krishnamurti replied: 'There is nothing permanent either on earth or in ourselves,' and explained how thought and memory create the illusion of permanence as a refuge from fear of the unknown. Returning to the woman's situation, he urged her to concern herself with the upbringing of her remaining children instead of with her own misery and self-pity. If she saw the absurdity of these feelings, he said, 'then you will naturally stop crying, stop isolating yourself, and live with the children with a new light and with a smile on your face.'[9]

Many religious books are concerned with instructing people

how to die, and on another occasion in India Krishnamurti was asked 'How can we learn to die?' and he replied, 'I say first learn how to live.'[15] When a person really learns how to live, Krishnamurti maintains, death ceases to be a problem for him and he does not seek solace in some concept of survival. Nor does he fear death. People may fear what they know, but to fear the unknown is illogical and foolish, and death is, supremely, the unknown. Fear of death, then, is not really fear of the unknown, but of losing the known. We tend to think of death, if we think of it at all, as a monstrous thing waiting to pounce upon us at the end of life's journey, but if we bring it closer, if we understand that it is an integral part of life and living and that there is nothing permanent except life itself, and if we learn in our living continually to die to the old in order to enable the new to exist, we do not fear death.

Religions generally postulate some kind of continuity as the answer to the question of death, offering believers the prospect of reincarnation, resurrection, or survival in some form which, although non-corporeal, is somehow capable of sensory contact with the physical world. But Krishnamurti argues, thinking in terms of continuity is thinking in terms of time. 'Continuity can be ended ... continuity is duration, and that which is everlasting is not the timeless.' The only kind of immortality we can have is in emancipation from time, which is a creation of thought. 'Thought, memory, is continuous through word and repetition. The ending of thought is the beginning of the new; the death of thought is life eternal. There must be constant ending for the new to be. That which is new is not continuous; the new can never be within the field of time. The new is only in death from moment to moment.'[4]

Here we come back to the experience of primary importance in Krishnamurti's life and philosophy: the experience of the death of the self. 'What is the thing that dies?'[18] he asks. The body dies of course, but that is such a palpable fact that people generally accept it, although they do not so easily accept the ending of the individual personality, the self. If, however, we are persuaded by Krishnamurti's analysis that the self is an inconsequential and rather arbitrary thing, a creation of environment, time, thought and memory, and if through that understanding or through some experience we are able to free ourselves from the concept of the self, then we will understand what death is and will not be afraid of it. We will learn to see it, as Krishnamurti does, as 'a great act of purgation',[18] as a liberation from the ephemeral pleasures, sorrows and attachments of what we call living. 'Can I live with death all the time?' Krishnamurti asks, and he explains how it is possible and the consequences of such a mode of living:

> I am attached to you; end that attachment, which is death – is it not? One is greedy , and when one dies one cannot carry greed with one; so end the greed, not in a week's time or ten days' time – end it now. So one is living a life full of vigour, energy, capacity, observation, seeing the beauty of the earth and also the ending of that instantly, which is death. So to live before death is to live with death; which means that one is living in a timeless world.[18]

# V

## *The Psychological Revolution*

Krishnamurti has lived through a time and in a world of unprecedented social and political turmoil. He has seen wars and revolutions claim millions of human lives, witnessed social and technological changes bewilder people in the present and make them fear for the future, and, particularly in his native India, has observed societies in the throes of self-destruction through their rigid adherence to traditional modes of thought and conduct. A lot has been said and written in his lifetime about new societies, brave new worlds, utopias, total revolutions, and in many places in the world ideas as to how these fundamental changes might be achieved have been put into practice. Such changes as there have been, however, have been superficial; brave new worlds have all too often turned out to be the flip-side of the bad old worlds and to have a tendency to flip back, and for all our efforts and awareness there has been no alleviation of human suffering and misery, no mitigation of human destructiveness, cruelty and stupidity during recent decades, and today there is as much alarmist talk about the end of the world or of human civilization as there ever has been, and not without reason.

In the early 1950s Krishnamurti was asked why he thought that the crisis in the world at that time was exceptional. He gave three reasons. First, because world conflicts were not over territorial or economic issues, but were over ideas, and ideologues were the most ruthless murderers who would make or demand any sacrifice in the cause of their chimerical ideal. Second, because man and the value of human life had ceased to be important to world political leaders, who could contemplate with equanimity the destruction of millions of people if they could see political advantage in it. And third, because of the exaggerated importance that man was giving to material values and particularist loyalties, for such a mental attitude was at the basis of human violence and hatred. These circumstances, Krishnamurti said, constituted an unprecedented crisis which demanded an unprecedented solution; nothing less than a psychological revolution, a fundamental change in the human mind and nature.

Revolution is a key term in Krishnamurti's philosophy. What people generally call revolution, he argues, is merely modified continuity, however much blood is shed and suffering undergone in the cause of it. Revolutions involving changes in political systems inevitably fail, 'because a system cannot transform man; man always transforms the system, which history shows.'[2] Gradual political reform, as distinct from revolution, is also unavailing because reform always needs further reform, and is an endless process 'like trying to clean the water in a tank which is constantly being filled with dirty water'.[2] Revolution based on religious beliefs and dogmas must also fail because it involves the exercise of authority and the denial of freedom, and thus engenders conflict, both in the individual and in society, which only makes confusion worse confounded. So is revolution itself a chimera? Is it unrealistic to look for change? Must we not accept man's unregenerate nature and leave the matter to God, meanwhile living as moral and honest a life as we can in the circumstances?

Of course, Krishnamurti does not propose such a resigned and negative attitude. He believes that a revolution is not only essential but also possible. He does not minimize the problems. Indeed, he believes that 'our problems – social, environmental, political, religious – are so complex that we can only solve them by being simple ... These problems demand a new approach; and they can be so approached only when we are simple, inwardly really simple.'[2] This simplicity that he advocates is not simple-mindedness or stupidity, but the ridding of the mind of all the ideas and so-called knowledge that block the direct perception and experience of reality. 'Our social structure is very intellectual,' he writes; 'we are cultivating the intellect at the expense of every other factor of our being and therefore we are suffocated with ideas.'[12]

But problems do not yield to attack by ideas, because ideas prevent us seeing a problem in its entirety and in all its ramifications, and it is only when there is such seeing and understanding that change comes about, and this involves being simple in Krishnamurti's sense of the term. In another context he speaks of poverty rather than simplicity, and says: 'It is important to be poor, not only in the things of the world, but also in belief and knowledge. A man with worldly riches or a man rich in knowledge and belief will never know anything but darkness, and will be the centre of all mischief and misery.'²

Murder, war, genocide, starvation, child-abuse, torture, and violence of all kinds are things that we all know occur in the world. We deplore and abhor them, but most of us do not feel in any way associated with them or responsible for them. We distance them, see them as things that occur 'out there', in a world incomprehensible to us in its inhumanity. And of course proportionately few of us have ever been directly involved in these things. But Krishnamurti insists that we are all involved and responsible, that the outside world is as it is because of what we inwardly are. 'If we are petty, jealous, vain, greedy – *that* is what we create about us, *that* is the society in which we live.'¹² The atrocities and stupidities perpetrated by nations and faiths may be writ so large that they seem something different from the little meannesses and follies of the individual, but the difference is of degree not of kind, and it is at the level of the individual life that all the trouble starts; there is no other reality, no malevolent devil urging man to do evil against his better nature.

Human qualities and characteristics become manifest in relationships, and human societies are complexes of relationships, so it is in relationships that we can see how things have gone wrong and possibly seek to make them go right. Krishnamurti writes: 'If you and I do not understand ourselves, merely transforming the outer, which is a projection of the inner, has no significance whatsoever; that is, there can be no significant alteration or modification in society so long as I do not understand myself in relationship to you. Being confused in my relationship, I create a society which is the replica, the outward expression of what I am.'² So the only revolution that could change the world is a revolution in the individual and in his attitudes to and conduct in his relationships, not only with other people but also with things, with nature, and with ideas.

Relationships must be vital, which means that they must be

sustained by an investment of energy. Mechanical energy is
subject to the law of entropy, it runs down, the operations it
governs become increasingly random, and ultimately it results
in a static state. This is an established fact of physical science,
and it applies by analogy to society and the relationships
which constitute it. If those relationships are sustained by
habit, tradition, pragmatic or politic considerations
formulated by thought, then they are mechanical, subject to
randomness, and will settle in a static form. But science
recognizes another kind of energy than the mechanical, which
is 'negentropic', that is to say, it does not run down but goes
on indefinitely and supports increasingly complex organic
structures. This is the fundamental life energy, and when it
functions in relationships it makes those relationships vital
instead of mechanical, and that vitality invests the social
structure that the complex of relationships comprises.

In a key passage, Krishnamurti puts it this way:

> To bring about a society that is not repetitive, not static, not
> disintegrating, a society that is constantly alive, it is imperative
> that there should be a revolution in the psychological structure of
> the individual, for without inward, psychological revolution, mere
> transformation of the outer has little significance ... Outward
> action, when accomplished, is over, is static; if the relationship
> between individuals, which is society, is not the outcome of
> inward revolution, then the social structure, being static, absorbs
> the individual and therefore makes him equally static, repetitive
> ... It is a fact that society is always crystallizing and absorbing
> the individual and that constant, creative revolution can only be
> in the individual, not in the outer. That is, creative revolution can
> take place only in individual relationship, which is society.[2]

A vital relationship is a relationship in which there is love.
Krishnamurti often speaks and writes about love, and the
term is central in his thinking about the psychological
revolution, so let us see what he means by it.

In attempting to define love, Krishnamurti proceeds by way
of stating what it is not, because 'as love is the unknown, we
must come at it by discarding the known'.[2] He first rejects the
love that is possessive, for it gives rise to jealousy, fear and
conflict. Then he considers whether to love is to be emotional
and sentimental, and he rejects the idea because he regards
emotion and sentimentality as merely forms of self-expansion,

and points out that when emotion is frustrated or sentiment is not responded to, a person may became cruel and violent, even towards the person he professes to love. The next supposed loving quality to come under scrutiny is forgiveness, and Krishnamurti rejects the claim of the forgiving person to be loving on the grounds that to say 'I forgive you' is to give undue importance to the 'I', to make the self the important figure in the situation. Forgiveness, sympathy, sentiment, possessiveness, jealousy, are all of the mind, and 'as long as the mind is the arbiter, there is no love.' But 'when these things disappear, when these things don't occupy your mind and when the things of the mind don't fill your heart, then there is love; and love alone can transform the present madness and insanity in the world.'[2]

Love, in other words, only comes into being with the death of the self. It is not a creation or activity of the self, not something that we can practise or cultivate, and above all it is not something that seeks results, for such seeking is a function of the mind, of the self, and it implies time, and love is not of time or of the self. But although it does not seek results, it is the only thing that can vitalize the relationships of which society is built up, and therefore the only thing that can produce the result of transforming society.

Of course, much of this has been said before. The poet W.H. Auden put it even more plainly than Krishnamurti when he wrote the line: 'We must love one another or die.' Auden was a Christian poet, and of course this is the basic Christian message. But Krishnamurti does not merely prescribe in vague terms the remedy for the world's ills; he goes into precise detail as to how the psychological revolution might come about. And here we come to what is most original and most contentious in his teaching: the claim that the change can be virtually instantaneous.

One of the most positive and encouraging developments in Western societies over recent years has been the increasing momentum of the 'human potentials' movement. The movement comprises numerous organizations and individuals advocating various means of promoting human spiritual growth and the full use of latent potentials, and although it has its fringe of faddists and fools it does reflect a widespread awareness of the need for radical change both in the individual and in society, and undoubtedly many people have profited by it, in that they have learnt to live what they consider to be more fulfilling and meaningful lives. Krishnamurti, however, looks rather askance at this movement, because he does not believe that radical psychological change is a cumulative process, the outcome of a programme of growth. He is not an evolutionist, he is a revolutionist. 'Transformation is not in the future ... It can only be *now*,'[2] he writes. 'Regeneration is today, not tomorrow.'[2] All means of seeking and working at change are activities of the self; but radical change is not a matter of the self becoming something other, but of the self coming to an end, and that has to happen instantaneously.

How does it happen? Krishnamurti has returned to this question many times over the years, and *à propos* it has developed his thoughts on 'the art of seeing'. He asks, 'What do we mean by transformation?' and answers: 'Surely it is very simple: seeing the false as the false and the true as the true. Seeing the truth in the false and seeing the false in that which has been accepted as truth. Seeing the false as the false and the true as the true is transformation, because when you see something very clearly as the truth, that truth liberates. When you see that something is false, that false thing drops away.'[2]

In this passage, seeing could be read as synonymous with understanding. But elsewhere Krishnamurti makes it quite clear that the seeing that leads to transformation is also seeing in the quite literal sense of the term. To observe, he says, 'is quite an art to which one must give a good deal of attention.' We only see very partially, we never see anything completely, with the totality of our mind, or with the fullness of our heart. Conditioning, concern with our own problems, our tendency to conceptualize, to form images of people and things and thereafter see the image instead of the reality, all prevent our direct perception of *what is*. Also our training and cultural background have taught us to see fragmentarily, analytically, to see the parts separately rather than the whole they constitute as a totality. This kind of seeing leads to dullness and insensitivity, to the mentality capable of exploiting or hurting the part because it does not see it in relation to the whole.

Total, clear, unimpeded seeing is rare; as rare, indeed, as love. In fact in a sense it is love, for genuine love cannot exist without it. In such seeing there is no barrier between the observer and the observed. People who have taken drugs, particularly LSD, have experienced this breaking down of barriers, or contraction of the space between observer and observed. But, says Krishnamurti, it is not necessary to take drugs. 'There is a much simpler, more direct, more natural way, which is to observe for yourself a tree, a flower, the face of a person; to look at any one of them, and so to look that the space between you and them is non-existent. And you can only look that way when there is love.'[13]

As with seeing, so with listening. 'Listen to the birds, listen to your wife's voice, however irritating, beautiful or ugly, listen to it and listen to your own voice however beautiful, ugly, or impatient it may be. Then out of this listening you will find that all separation between the observer and the observed comes to an end.'[13] Listening and seeing are modes of attention. Attention is another word that Krishnamurti uses with special significance. We speak of paying attention, and, largely as a result of our schooling, we think of attention as a disciplining of the mind, forcing it to concentrate on a particular thing to the exclusion of other things, resisting distraction. We tend to think that the mind can only be in one of two states, either wandering, open to all kinds of vagrant thoughts and impressions, or concentrated, absorbed by one thing.

Krishnamurti maintains that these are not the only possible mental states, that there is another mode of attention which is not absorbed and exclusive. Being absorbed, forcing attention and resisting distraction, are things that misuse energy which would be better applied to unforced and non-exclusive attention. Such attention *is* discipline. The Latin root of the word discipline, Krishnamurti reminds us, means to learn and learning is not something forced but something accomplished through observation. For the mind which is constantly aware, choicelessly, which is attentive and responsive to impressions from the totality of its environment from moment to moment, learning is a natural and continuous process. Truth is accessible to such a mind, but it is not accessible to the mind that is concentrated on one thing, even if that thing is the pursuit of truth, or to the mind that is crammed with knowledge, belief and experience.

In the human potentials movement there are many purveyors of techniques of meditation and mind control, and

Krishnamurti has observed with a certain amusement the
success and popularity they have enjoyed in recent years.
'Unfortunately,' he told one of his audiences, 'people come
from the East with their systems, methods and so on; they say
"Do this" and "Don't do that", "Practise Zen and you will
find enlightenment." Some of you may have gone to India or
Japan and spent years studying, disciplining yourself, trying
to become aware of your toe or nose, practising endlessly. Or
you may have repeated certain words in order to calm the
mind, so that in that calmness there will be the perception of
something beyond thought. These tricks can be practised by a
very stupid, dull mind. I am using the word stupid in the sense
of a mind that is stupefied. A stupefied mind can practise any
of these tricks.'[11]

These 'tricks' are supposed to be systems of meditation,
but, says Krishnamurti, 'a system implies practice, following,
repetition, changing "what actually is" and therefore
increasing your conflict. Systems make the mind mechanical,
they don't give you freedom, they may promise freedom at the
end, but freedom is at the beginning not at the end.'[13]

To practise meditation for the purpose of self-improvement,
in the hope of advancing spiritually, or of becoming a more
relaxed person, and therefore happier and more efficient,
involves pursuing aims in time, but real meditation is a way of
being, not of becoming, and it is impossible for a mind that is
seeking results. 'Freedom is at the beginning,' says
Krishnamurti, and elsewhere he states that 'the first step is the
last step.' He does not offer a technique for bringing about the
instantaneous psychological transformation in the individual
that he maintains is the only revolution that will see the world
through its present crisis, but what he has to say about
meditation gives clear guidance on the subject and is really the
very essence of his teaching. 'A psychological revolution is
absolutely necessary for a different kind of world, a different
kind of society, to come into being,' he has written; and 'that
revolution can only take place at the very centre of our being
and requires a great abundance of energy; meditation is the
release of that total energy.'[2]

People who meditate according to prescribed systems or
methods usually set apart certain times of day for the practice
and do it under special conditions. But, Krishnamurti says,
meditation has no beginning and no end, it is not something

done outside the conditions of daily life, and it is not something that you can do deliberately. 'Don't look out of the window hoping to catch it unawares, or sit in a darkened room waiting for it; it comes only when you are not there at all, and its bliss has no continuity.'[8]

Krishnamurti is emphatic about what meditation is not. It is not an escape from the world, it is not 'the repetition of a word, nor the experience of a vision, nor the cultivation of silence ... not wrapping yourself in a pattern of thought, in the enchantment of pleasures.'[8] It is not prayer, for the prayer that is supplication is born of self-pity, which is rooted in the sense of separateness, and in the meditative experience there is no separateness, there is wholeness and union with the entire movement of life. And it is not a way or a path to anything; certainly not to freedom, for freedom is the precondition of true meditation.

Krishnamurti certainly does not make it easy for anyone who wishes to embark on the work which he stresses is essential to the world's survival. But while he insists that there is no 'how' of meditation, his talks and writings are, paradoxically, full of indications as to the conditions and attitudes conducive to meditation in his sense of the term. Perhaps he is least ambiguous about it when he is talking to children. In one such talk he told his audience:

You have to watch, as you watch a lizard going by, walking across the wall, seeing all its four feet, how it sticks to the wall, you have to watch it, and as you watch, you see all the movement, the delicacy of its movements, So in the same way, watch your thinking, do not correct, do not suppress it – do not say it is too hard – just watch it, now, this morning.[21]

The basis of meditation, then, is watchfulness, both of the objective and of the subjective worlds. It is 'seeing, watching, listening, without word, without comment, without opinion – attentive to the movement of life in all its relationships throughout the day.'[8] It is the continual emptying of the mind of thought and experience, allowing the stream of consciousness to flow freely without thought seizing on any of its elements; it is living and dying from moment to moment.

Another paradox about it is that although it is not a thing you can deliberately set out to do, it nevertheless demands hard work and 'the highest form of discipline – not

conformity, not imitation, not obedience, but a discipline
which comes through constant awareness, not only of the
things about you outwardly, but also inwardly.'⁸ Just watch
and be aware of all your thoughts, feelings and reactions,
without judging, comparing, approving, condemning or
evaluating them in any way, Krishnamurti says. Try it, do it,
he urges, and you will find that there is a tremendous release
of energy, there is the opening of the door into spaciousness,
there is the awakening of bliss.

In a telling image he likens the bliss of meditation to a pure
flame, and thought to the smoke from a fire which brings tears
to the eyes and blurs perception. In meditation the mind
penetrates and understands the entire structure of the self and
the world that thought has put together, and the very act of
seeing and understanding the structure confers freedom from
it, for meditation 'destroys everything, nothing whatsoever is
left, and in this vast, unfathomable emptiness there is creation
and love.'⁶

# Bibliography

## Books by Krishnamurti

1. *Early Writings*, Chetana, Bombay, 1969.
2. *The First and Last Freedom*, Victor Gollancz, London, 1954.
3. *Commentaries on Living: First Series*, Victor Gollancz, London, 1956.
4. *Commentaries on Living: Second Series*, Victor Gollancz, London, 1959.
5. *Commentaries on Living: Third Series*, Victor Gollancz, London, 1961.
6. *This Matter of Culture*, Victor Gollancz, London, 1964.
7. *Freedom from the Known*, Victor Gollancz, London, 1969.
8. *The Only Revolution*, Victor Gollancz, London, 1970.
9. *Talks and Dialogues*, Avon Books, N.Y., 1970.
10. *The Urgency of Change*, Victor Gollancz, London, 1971.
11. *The Impossible Question*, Victor Gollancz, London, 1972.
12. *You Are the World*, Harper and Row, N.Y., 1972.
13. *The Awakening of Intelligence*, Victor Gollancz, London, 1973.
14. *Beginnings of Learning*, Victor Gollancz, London, 1975.
15. *Tradition and Revolution*, Sangam Books, Madras, 1975.
16. *Krishnamurti's Notebook*, Victor Gollancz, London, 1976.
17. *Truth and Actuality*, Victor Gollancz, London, 1977.
18. *The Wholeness of Life*, Victor Gollancz, London, 1978.

## Books and Essays on Krishnamurti

19. Dhopeshwarkar, A.D., *Krishnamurti and the Experience of the Silent Mind*, Chetana, Bombay, 1956.
20. Dhopeshwarkar, A.D., *Krishnamurti and the Mind in Revolution*, Chetana, Bombay, 1971.
21. Goleman, Daniel, *Krishnamurti's Choiceless Awareness* (in Goleman, *The Varieties of Meditative Experience*, Dutton, N.Y., 1977).
22. Lutyens, Mary, *Krishnamurti: The Years of Awakening*, Farrar, Straus & Giroux, N.Y., 1975.
23. Methorst-Kuiper, A.J.G., *Krishnamurti*, Chetana, Bombay, 1971.

24. Needleman, Jacob, *A Note on Krishnamurti* (In Needleman, *The New Religions*, Doubleday, N.Y., 1970).
25. Niel, Andre, *Krishnamurti: The Man in Revolt*, Chetana, Bombay, 1957.
26. Suares, Carlo, *Krishnamurti and the Unity of Man*, Chetana, Bombay, 1953.
27. Vas, Luis S.R., (ed.) *The Mind of J. Krishnamurti*, Jaico Publishing House, Bombay, 1971.
28. Weeraperuma, Susanaga, *Living and Dying from Moment to Moment*, Chetana, Bombay, 1978.

*Index*

# Index

Dream— Monkey paws
as tossing entrails